JAPANESE COMBINED FLEET 1942–43

Guadalcanal to the Solomons Campaign

Mark Stille
Illustrated by Jim Laurier

OSPREY PUBLISHING
Bloomsbury Publishing Plc
Kemp House, Chawley Park, Cumnor Hill, Oxford OX2 9PH, UK
29 Earlsfort Terrace, Dublin 2, Ireland
1385 Broadway, 5th Floor, New York, NY 10018, USA
E-mail: info@ospreypublishing.com
www.ospreypublishing.com

OSPREY is a trademark of Osprey Publishing Ltd

First published in Great Britain in 2024

© Osprey Publishing Ltd, 2024

All rights reserved. No part of this publication may be reproduced or transmitted in any form or by any means, electronic or mechanical, including photocopying, recording, or any information storage or retrieval system, without prior permission in writing from the publishers.

A catalog record for this book is available from the British Library.

ISBN: PB 9781472860491; eBook 9781472860521; ePDF 9781472860507; XML 9781472860514

24 25 26 27 28 10 9 8 7 6 5 4 3 2 1

Maps by bounford.com
Diagrams by Adam Tooby
Index by Fionbar Lyons
Typeset by PDQ
Printed and bound in India by Repro India Ltd.

Front Cover: Art by Jim Laurier
Osprey Publishing supports the Woodland Trust, the UK's leading woodland conservation charity.

To find out more about our authors and books visit www.ospreypublishing.com. Here you will find extracts, author interviews, details of forthcoming events and the option to sign up for our newsletter.

CONTENTS

THE FLEET'S PURPOSE   4
    The Combined Fleet's South Pacific Campaign

FLEET FIGHTING POWER   15
    The Ships
    Technical Factors

HOW THE FLEET OPERATED   31
    Doctrine and Command
    Intelligence, Communication and Deception
    Logistics and Facilities

COMBAT AND ANALYSIS   52
    The Fleet in Combat
    Analysis

FURTHER READING   79

INDEX   80

THE FLEET'S PURPOSE

During the first six months of the war, the Imperial Japanese Navy (IJN) enjoyed an unrivaled string of successes, up until May 1942. However, in the battle of the Coral Sea (May 4–8), the Combined Fleet – the main fighting force of the IJN – fought its first battle against strong Allied forces and suffered a tactical and strategic defeat. This set the stage for the battle of Midway, fought between June 4 and 6, 1942. In what is (incorrectly) viewed as the single most decisive battle of the Pacific War, the Combined Fleet's Striking Force suffered the loss of four fleet carriers. Since Japan began the war with only six fleet carriers, this had the effect of blunting the IJN's offensive power. Before the Japanese could react to this new dynamic, the United States Navy (USN) grabbed the initiative in the Pacific and launched an offensive at Guadalcanal in the southern Solomon Islands.

The first American offensive of World War II prompted a grinding six-month battle of attrition between August 1942 and February 1943 before the Japanese were forced to retreat from Guadalcanal. During this contest, the IJN suffered heavy losses in aircraft, aircrew, and ships. In the ensuing campaign for the Central and Northern Solomons, the IJN was forced into force preservation mode. Not until November 1943 did the then Commander of the Combined Fleet, Admiral Koga Mineichi, decide it was possible and necessary to commit major fleet units and precious carrier aircraft to defend Bougainville in the Northern Solomons. This book details how the Combined Fleet fought the Guadalcanal and Solomons campaigns and examines why these were so critical to Japanese naval fortunes for the remainder of the war.

THE COMBINED FLEET'S SOUTH PACIFIC CAMPAIGN

Japanese objectives in the First Operational Phase included Rabaul on the island of New Britain in the South Pacific. In January 1942, the Japanese occupied

Rabaul against minimal Australian resistance. With its large harbor and several airfields, Rabaul thereafter became the principal Japanese base in the South Pacific. The Japanese sought to create more operational depth for the defense of their new conquests during the Second Operational Phase. The list of Second Operational Phase objectives was ambitious: the Aleutian Islands in the North Pacific, Midway Atoll in the Central Pacific, and eastern New Guinea, the Fijis, Samoa, and "strategic points in the Australian area" in the South Pacific. Because the IJN lacked the forces and shipping to conduct operations against these widespread objectives in anything like a concurrent timeline, operations had to be carefully sequenced. Planning was further complicated by the fact that the IJN and the Imperial Japanese Army (IJA) had competing strategic priorities. Differences between the IJN and the IJA were especially evident with regards to the South Pacific, where the IJA refused to write a blank check to support the IJN's future offensive operations.

Even within the IJN there were severe differences on the shape of future expansion. The Commander of the Combined Fleet, Fleet Admiral Yamamoto Isoroku, wanted to give priority to the Central Pacific thrust. He planned an attack against Midway Atoll to draw out the remaining units of the USN's Pacific Fleet, whereupon they would be destroyed. The Naval General Staff preferred an immediate advance into the South Pacific to cut the sea lines of communications (SLOC) between the United States and Australia. The IJA made it clear that it would not commit large ground forces in the region, ruling out any attack on Australia. However, it was willing to support operations against key South Pacific islands.

During the first week of April 1942, the Naval General Staff and the Combined Fleet reached an uneasy compromise on the phasing of future operations. Yamamoto used the threat of resignation to get his Midway plan approved. This also required a compromise in which the Combined Fleet would conduct a series of tightly sequenced operations in the South Pacific in early May, followed by the main operation against Midway in June. An additional compromise was that an operation against the Aleutians was scheduled concurrently with the Midway operation.

Special Type destroyer *Amigiri* is a good example of the operational tempo of Combined Fleet destroyers during the Guadalcanal and Solomons campaigns. It made 11 runs to Guadalcanal. During the Solomons campaign, among its many operations it participated in the battle of Kula Gulf in July 1943. The following month, it earned perpetual notoriety by ramming and sinking *PT-109*, commanded by future President John F. Kennedy while on a transport run to Kolombangara. (Naval History and Heritage Command)

SOUTH PACIFIC BASES

South Pacific operations scheduled for May included an amphibious operation to seize Port Moresby on New Guinea and the occupation of Tulagi Island in the Southern Solomons. Preparations for the Combined Fleet's offensive into the South Pacific were detected by the Americans, and the USN was able to send two carriers to the region. In the resulting battle of the Coral Sea on May 7 and 8, 1942, the Combined Fleet suffered its first strategic defeat of the war. All three Japanese carriers involved were either sunk or placed out of action, forcing the cancellation of the Port Moresby invasion. The only success for the Japanese was the occupation of Tulagi on May 3, which gave the Japanese their first toehold in the Southern Solomons.

Not only did the Port Moresby operation fail, but the cost of the failure imperiled Yamamoto's larger operation against Midway and the Aleutians. Excessive force dispersion and sloppy planning on every level contributed to the defeat at Midway, where four Japanese fleet carriers were sunk or disabled on June 4. Losses of this magnitude impacted future Japanese plans in the South Pacific. Operations to occupy New Caledonia, the Fijis, and Samoa were postponed on June 11, then permanently cancelled in July. However, the Japanese were not totally passive. Only 20 miles to the south of Tulagi was the largely unknown island of Guadalcanal. On June 13, the Japanese decided to build an airfield on its northern coast. On July 6, a 12-ship convoy arrived off Lunga Point on Guadalcanal with two IJN construction units. Work proceeded quickly, with completion of the airfield expected in August.

Disaster at Midway forced the Japanese to assume a defensive posture in the South Pacific. The Americans, driven by Admiral Ernest King, Commander in Chief US Fleet, were determined to use the victory at Midway to grab the initiative and begin offensive operations in the South Pacific. The initial targets were Guadalcanal and Tulagi, with the final objective being the occupation of Rabaul. On June 24, King ordered Admiral Chester Nimitz, Commander of the US Pacific Fleet, to begin planning on attack to recapture Tulagi. After American intelligence assessed that an airfield was being built on Guadalcanal, the island was added as an objective on July 5. On August 7, Marines landed on Tulagi and Guadalcanal. Tulagi was secured after sharp fighting, and by the following day Marines had captured the unfinished airfield on Guadalcanal.

Plans and Planning at Guadalcanal

The ultimate Japanese objective during the campaign was to eliminate the Marines on Guadalcanal and defeat the USN in the process. From the very beginning, the Japanese were handicapped by poor intelligence which

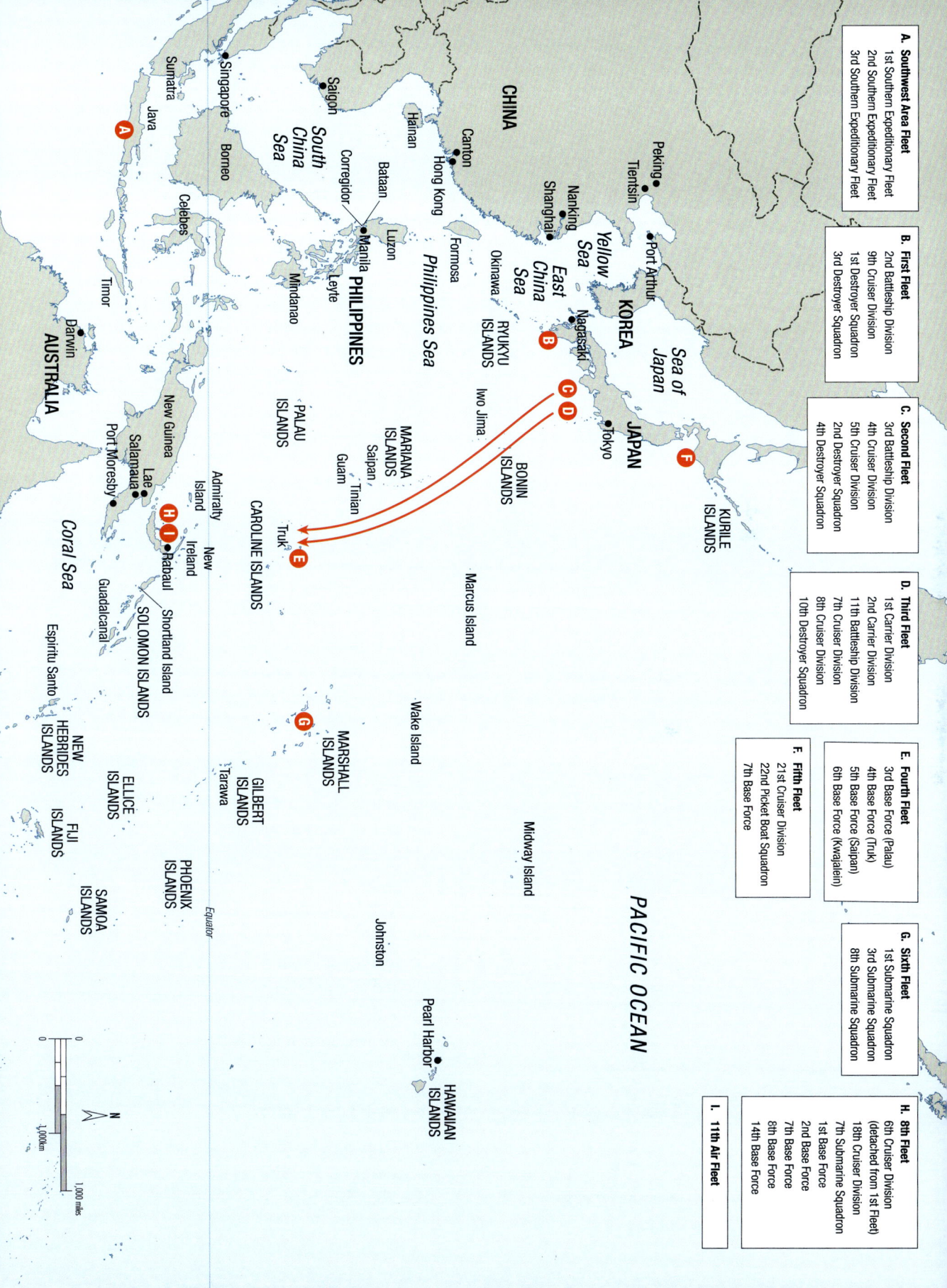

Chokai pictured in the Truk anchorage in October 1942. Behind it is a Yamato-class battleship. *Chokai* served as Eighth Fleet's flagship during the Guadalcanal campaign and was present at Savo Island. It returned to Guadalcanal on October 14 to bombard Henderson Field and took part in another bombardment on November 14. (Yamato Museum)

consistently underestimated the size of the American garrison on the island. Another complicating factor was the different perspectives of the IJN and the IJA. The IJN's focus was destroying USN forces, not retaking the island, which it viewed as the IJA's problem.

Upon learning of the American invasion, Vice-Admiral Mikawa Gunichi, commander of the Eighth Fleet based at Rabaul, assembled whatever forces were available for an immediate counterattack. This quick response resulted in a significant Japanese victory in the battle of Savo Island, fought on the night of August 8. Having satisfied his goal of sinking American ships, Mikawa made no effort to follow up his victory by attacking the invasion force. This was a critical error; more mistakes were to follow. The American defeat at Savo Island and the apparent absence of activity in the beachhead led the Japanese to assess that most of the Marines had withdrawn from Guadalcanal, leaving only a small, demoralized garrison.

The initial Japanese ground attack on the night of August 20–21, conducted with only a battalion, met with total disaster. Concurrently, Yamamoto moved the Combined Fleet to the South Pacific to mount an operation to crush the American fleet off Guadalcanal. With the rebuilt carrier force leading the way, the result was the indecisive carrier clash at the battle of the Eastern Solomons on August 24. Not only did the Combined Fleet fail to crush the USN, but it failed to get a small reinforcement convoy to the island. With the arrival of American aircraft at what was named Henderson Field, the Japanese were faced with a much more complex problem of how to defeat the American garrison on Guadalcanal. American air units on Guadalcanal played a lead role in turning back the Japanese reinforcement convoy on August 25.

Yamamoto and his Combined Fleet staff learned a critical lesson from their August defeat – the American airfield on Guadalcanal was the key to the entire campaign and had to be neutralized. American aircraft flying from Henderson

Field made it impossible to operate naval units within range of the airfield during the day. The most important implication of this was that the only method to move IJA forces to the island was by nightly destroyer runs, the so-called "Tokyo Express" (called "Rat Transportation" by the Japanese). Operating from the anchorage at Shortland Island on the southern tip of Bougainville, destroyers made a high-speed approach to Guadalcanal at dusk and arrived off the island at night. Once off the island, the destroyers quickly unloaded troops and supplies, then made a high-speed dash back toward Shortland to get out of range of Henderson Field before dawn. This tactic was successful in avoiding air attack, since American aircraft typically did not fly at night.

Relying on destroyer runs to move large numbers of troops was an extremely inefficient process. A typical load was limited to 40–50 tons of materiel on deck and some 150 troops. There was not enough space on deck to carry vehicles, tanks, or heavy artillery. Getting enough men, heavy equipment, and supplies to Guadalcanal required slow transports, but to do this the Japanese had to achieve air superiority.

By conducting almost nightly destroyer runs, by mid-September the Combined Fleet had moved the equivalent of a reinforced brigade to the island. This force conducted its attack on two consecutive nights between September 12 and 14, with the objective of seizing the airfield. Once again, the Marines stopped the assault and inflicted heavy losses on the attackers.

After the September defeat, both the IJN and IJA began to take the Guadalcanal campaign more seriously. Both services agreed that Guadalcanal was shaping up as a decisive battle, and therefore decisive forces were required for victory. To finish the job, the IJA planned to move two divisions to the island. To get such a large force to Guadalcanal in time to conduct the attack planned for October 20, destroyer runs were insufficient. The Combined Fleet was forced to come up with new approaches to suppress Henderson Field. Land-based air forces based at Rabaul had been charged with this responsibility since August 20, when the Americans began operations from Henderson Field, but had failed. There were several reasons for this, including the distance from Rabaul to Guadalcanal which decreased the frequency and effectiveness of raids, the lack of sufficient numbers of aircraft, and the ineffectiveness of Japanese bombers and their escorts in a counter-air role.

With Henderson Field still fully functional despite the efforts of Japanese land-based air forces, the Combined Fleet came up with another approach. For the first time, the objective of recapturing the island was placed above that of defeating American naval forces. This was reflected in a plan to use heavy ships to bombard the airfield and place it out of action. The first attempt to neutralize the airfield with a bombardment by three heavy cruisers was unsuccessful, when for the first time since the start of the campaign, the USN decided to contest the waters around Guadalcanal at night. In the resulting battle of Cape Esperance, the Japanese cruiser force was surprised and defeated.

THE CAMPAIGN FOR GUADALCANAL

Only a few nights later, the Combined Fleet tried again, this time with a battleship bombardment of the airfield. On the night of October 13–14, two battleships conducted a bombardment of Henderson Field. The effects were devastating, resulting in the only serious suppression of Henderson Field during the campaign. Temporarily neutralizing the airfield allowed the Japanese to move a transport convoy to the island for the first time. Combined with intensified Tokyo Express runs, the IJA now had a reinforced division on the island and could plan another offensive to take the airfield.

For their October attack, the IJA chose the same axis used for the September assault. However, the attack was uncoordinated and was defeated by the Marines over two nights between October 24 and 26. The largest IJA ground attack of the campaign led to the largest IJN operation since Midway, including a force of five carriers. In the resulting battle of Santa Cruz fought on October 26, the IJN won its only carrier battle of the war. However, the cost of victory was high in terms of carrier aircrew and the Japanese were unable to exploit this victory. Critically, the Japanese falsely assessed that the American carrier force was neutralized for the remainder of the campaign.

Defeat in October at Guadalcanal drove Japan's Imperial Headquarters to a strategic consensus for the first time. The IJA now agreed with the IJN that the struggle for Guadalcanal was the decisive battle that both services had been seeking. The IJA believed that it had come close to victory in October, and the IJN believed it had sunk as many as four American carriers at Santa Cruz. Given this, it was thought that one more major effort would finally succeed in taking

Only four of the transports in Yamamoto's pivotal November convoy made it to Guadalcanal. The four surviving ships were ordered to beach on the island, but were quickly destroyed by air attack and gunfire from USN destroyers. *Yamazaki Maru* is pictured here after the battle in February 1943. The defeat of the November convoy spelled the end of Japanese attempts to recapture Guadalcanal. (Naval History and Heritage Command)

back the island and inflicting a major defeat on the Americans. For the final assault, the IJA and IJN planned to move another two divisions to the island.

Moving such a large force meant the Combined Fleet would have to redouble its efforts. Because land-based air forces from Rabaul were still unable to suppress Henderson Field, Yamamoto planned another battleship bombardment of the airfield. This prompted the decisive moment of the campaign. Over two nights between November 13 and 15, American naval forces defeated two Japanese attempts to obliterate Henderson Field with 14in. battleship guns. This failure allowed aircraft from Henderson Field, assisted by the USN's only operational fleet carrier, to destroy a large transport convoy headed for the island, sinking ten of 11 transports.

The scale of this defeat forced the Japanese to reevaluate their strategic objectives in the Solomons. Both the IJA and the IJN agreed that they were unable to withstand the cost of a renewed effort to recapture Guadalcanal, so agreed on a withdrawal from the island. American aircraft based on Guadalcanal, combined with a more aggressive naval blockade, meant that the Japanese were not even able to move sufficient supplies to the island to feed their troops. One of the final Tokyo Express runs to Guadalcanal resulted in the last major naval clash at the battle of Tassafaronga on the night of November 30. Though a stunning defeat for the USN, it did not change the desperate straits of the Japanese garrison on the island. In the final phase of the campaign, Yamamoto ordered that every effort be made to evacuate the emaciated Japanese survivors on Guadalcanal. On three nights during the first week of February, a total of 58 destroyer runs removed 10,652 men, bringing the campaign to a close.

The Solomons Campaign

By February 1943, Japan's position in the South Pacific had been seriously undermined. Guadalcanal had been lost, despite an all-out effort. The IJN had suffered such severe losses it was forced to disengage from the Guadalcanal campaign to save itself for a future decisive battle under better conditions. The IJN's air power, both carrier- and land-based, was also severely attrited and was never the factor it was earlier in the war. Following its defeat at Guadalcanal, the Combined Fleet's ability to contest a renewed American advance into the Central and Northern Solomons had been severely degraded.

Concurrent with the struggle for Guadalcanal, there was another campaign being waged on the Papuan Peninsula of New Guinea. Following the battle of the Coral Sea, which thwarted the Japanese plan to seize the Allied base of Port Moresby by sea, a small IJA force landed at Buna on the northeastern coast of the peninsula and tried to move to Port Moresby by land. The attack not only lacked proper logistical support, but was mounted over some of the most rugged terrain in the world. After the unsurprising failure of this operation, the Americans and Australians went over to the offensive to secure the Papuan

Yugumo-class destroyer *Naganami*, shown here in June 1942, was sent to the front immediately after being commissioned and saw heavy action from October 1942 until the end of the Guadalcanal campaign. In July 1943, it participated in the evacuation of Kiska in the Aleutians before moving back to the Solomons. It took part in the battle of Empress Augusta Bay. Following the battle, *Naganami* was heavily damaged by a torpedo during an attack on Simpson Harbor. (Yamato Museum)

Peninsula. Thus, the campaigns in Papua and the Solomons were linked throughout 1942 and 1943. Rabaul was the primary Japanese support hub for both campaigns, but Japanese naval and air forces operating from Rabaul were forced to support both campaigns against increasingly strong Allied air, naval, and ground forces.

Despite the loss of the Southern Solomons, the Japanese were determined to defend the rest of the Solomons. This was driven by a requirement to protect the major fleet base at Truk in the Central Pacific and the Philippines, which lay astride Japan's SLOCs with the occupied Dutch East Indies. Any defense of the Central and Northern Solomons was dependent on holding Rabaul. Friction between the IJN and the IJA often made planning difficult, but as early as November 1942 an agreement was reached for the Navy to take primary responsibility for the Solomons and the Army to focus on New Guinea. By mounting an "active defense" in the Solomons, forces could be shifted to New Guinea for offensive operations. Accordingly, all or parts of three IJA divisions were allocated to eastern New Guinea. Moving these forces and then resupplying them was a major task for the IJN.

Despite their lesser priority, Imperial General Headquarters ordered that both the Central and Northern Solomons be defended. The IJN decided that it would husband its principal naval units and use land-based air power and destroyer squadrons to defend the Central Solomons. This created friction with the IJA, which had just seen more than two divisions moved to Guadalcanal and then not supplied adequately. It believed that supplying forces in the Central Solomons would be too difficult. Accordingly, it wanted to give them up and defend Bougainville in the Northern Solomons. The IJN wanted to hold New Georgia in the Central Solomons to provide depth to the defense of Bougainville. On March 22, 1943, the IJA and IJN reached another compromise agreement that gave the IJA responsibility for the Northern Solomons and the IJN for the Central Solomons.

Haguro was one of two heavy cruisers that led the unsuccessful Combined Fleet attack against the American invasion fleet in Empress Augusta Bay. The scratch Japanese force performed poorly, the American commander making every effort to avoid being a target for Type 93s. The next morning, November 2, 1943, *Haguro* was caught in Simpson Harbor and attacked by USAAF bombers. This exceptionally clear combat photograph shows the cruiser in the foreground, with a burning transport to the right. (Naval History and Heritage Command)

When the Americans began their Central Solomons offensive, the IJN quickly turned to the IJA for more troops. After negotiations between the local IJA and IJN commanders, and in the spirit of the March 22 agreement, the IJA dispatched more forces to Kolombangara and New Georgia between May and July. This placed the IJN in a situation where it had to commit more light forces to move and support these troops and resulted in a series of night actions when USN forces attempted to interdict Japanese movements and resupply. The IJN's success in moving forces into the Central Solomons prolonged the struggle for New Georgia. Eventually, American forces cleared the island and built an airfield on it, giving them control of the Central Solomons.

On November 1, the Americans landed on Bougainville at Empress Augusta Bay on the west-central coast of the island. Once the Americans built airfields there, they would be less then 200nm from Rabaul. The IJN, assessing this was a mortal danger to Rabaul, prepared to commit major forces to attack the American beachhead. Koga was so concerned that he sent 173 carrier aircraft from Truk to Rabaul to attack the Americans. Two heavy cruisers which had arrived in Rabaul as part of a convoy escort were tasked to lead a major naval force to attack the American invasion force. This prompted the battle of Empress Augusta Bay, which ended in a Japanese defeat. After Admiral Koga learned of this setback, he decided to commit a much larger force to crush the beachhead. Seven heavy cruisers, one light cruiser, and four destroyers were ordered to move to Rabaul from Truk. This force was struck by American carrier aircraft in Simpson Harbor on November 5, and four heavy cruisers were damaged. This ended the Japanese naval threat to the Bougainville beachhead and was the last major IJN operation in the Solomons.

FLEET FIGHTING POWER

THE SHIPS

At the start of the Pacific War, the IJN enjoyed a slight numerical advantage compared to the combined Pacific forces of the USN and Royal Navy. Japanese naval losses were light during the first six months of the war (except in the critical category of aircraft carriers), so the Combined Fleet was still larger than the USN's Pacific Fleet in August 1942.

PACIFIC NAVAL STRENGTH AUGUST 1942					
	Carriers (fleet/light)	Battleships (new/old)	Heavy Cruisers	Light Cruisers	Destroyers (new/old)
IJN	4/3	1/10	17	17	67/39
USN	4/0	1/7	14	13	59/21

By the end of the Solomons campaign in November 1943, the scale of Japanese naval losses, combined with the flood of American naval production, served to tilt the naval balance firmly in the favor of the Americans. Not only did the Combined Fleet lose its quantitative advantage over this period, but it lost its qualitative edge as well.

Combined Fleet Aircraft Carriers

At the start of the war, the IJN possessed the largest carrier fleet in the world. Of the ten carriers in service in December 1941, six were fleet carriers. In the first six months of the war, the Combined Fleet lost five carriers. Four more carriers entered service during this period, so the Combined Fleet entered the Guadalcanal campaign with a total of nine.

JAPANESE FLEET AND LIGHT AIRCRAFT CARRIERS, JULY 1942–NOVEMBER 1943			
Available July 1942	Sunk July 1942–November 1943	New construction	In service November 1943
9	1	4	12

The overall number of Japanese carriers in service during this period presents a deceiving picture. Of the nine carriers active in July, only two were fleet carriers, the rest a collection of old ships or legacy conversions designed to circumvent prewar naval restrictions. In addition, two were escort carriers and were not considered by the Japanese as suitable for fleet work, being primarily used as aircraft ferries during this period of the war.

The centerpiece of the IJN's carrier force was the two ships of the Shokaku class. Designed without any treaty restrictions, these were excellent ships with a fine balance of protection, speed, and striking power. The Junyo class was a useful addition to the Combined Fleet when it entered service between May and July 1942. As conversions from large passenger liners, they were not as capable as fleet carriers, but were much larger and more capable than light carriers. Both ships were relatively slow and carried minimal protection, but their fairly large aircraft capacity made them useful additions to the fleet.

In addition to the two true fleet carriers and the two pseudo-fleet carriers, the Combined Fleet operated a diverse collection of light carriers. The oldest was *Hosho*, commissioned in December 1922. After taking part in the Midway operation, it was permanently assigned to training duties. Commissioned in 1933, *Ryujo* was an ambitious failure, an example of the IJN attempting to avoid treaty restrictions. When completed, it displaced some 12,500 tons – clearly over treaty limits. The ship possessed a nominal aircraft capacity of 48, but never carried that many in service.

Another method used by the IJN to circumvent treaty restrictions was the construction of auxiliaries designed to be easily converted into carriers. An example of this was the Shoho class. Laid down as submarine tenders, *Zuiho* was commissioned as a carrier in December 1940, and *Shoho* followed in January 1942. *Shoho* was sunk during the battle of the Coral Sea. Both ships were the most successful IJN light carrier conversions, each being able to carry 30 aircraft and possessing adequate speed to operate with the fleet carriers.

Ryuho, commissioned in November 1942, was converted from a submarine tender. With its low speed, it was considered the least effective light conversion. *Chiyoda* was commissioned in October 1943 after being converted from a

The heart of the Combined Fleet's carrier force after Midway were the two ships of the Shokaku class. This is *Shokaku* pictured after its commissioning in 1941. (Naval History and Heritage Command)

seaplane tender. Along with its sister *Chitose* (commissioned as a carrier in January 1944), it possessed capabilities comparable to *Zuiho*, both being useful additions to the fleet.

Four Japanese escort carriers were active during this period; all were converted from passenger ships. Unlike USN escort carriers, IJN escort carriers were not fitted with catapults, which restricted their operational usefulness. During this period of the war, all were used almost exclusively as aircraft transports. The first IJN escort carrier was *Taiyo*, commissioned in 1941, which was followed by two sister ships in 1942. *Kaiyo* was commissioned in November 1943 as a carrier.

Combined Fleet Battleships

Because of treaty restrictions, the IJN began the Pacific War with a battle line of only ten battleships. All ten were completed during or immediately after World War I, but had been modernized between the wars. With 15 older battleships, the USN possessed significantly more battleships and had an immense building program underway. The IJN intended to compensate for its numerical inferiority with a program to build superbattleships beginning in 1937.

JAPANESE BATTLESHIPS, JULY 1942–NOVEMBER 1943			
Available July 1942	Sunk July 1942–November 1943	New construction	In service November 1943
11	3	1	9

By far the most active Japanese battleships during the first six months of the war were the four ships of the Kongo class. Despite being the oldest of the IJN's battleships, they were also the fastest, which made them well suited to operate with the Striking Force. Two ships (and on one occasion four) were assigned to escort the carriers of the Striking Force. Though fast, the Kongo class was not well protected. Originally built as battlecruisers, beginning in 1911, they possessed inadequate protection despite being heavily modernized and reclassified as fast battleships. Their main battery of eight 14in. guns was mediocre compared to other battleships.

The second class of Japanese dreadnoughts was the two-ship Fuso class. *Fuso* entered service in 1915, followed by *Yamashiro* two years later. When completed, they provided another example of the IJN's emphasis on firepower – both ships were fitted with a main battery of 12 14in. guns. Both underwent modernization in the 1930s, but this did not fully address their weak protection, and in particular their poor underwater protection. Because they were considered second-line units, both remained in home waters until August 1943, when *Fuso* was used to ferry troops and supplies to Truk. *Yamashiro* was designated as a midshipmen training ship in September 1943.

Following the Midway debacle, the IJN looked for ways to replace its aircraft carrier losses. One method was to convert the two Ise-class battleships into hybrid carrier-battleships. This scheme involved removing the two after

Yamato and *Musashi* at anchor inside Truk lagoon sometime during 1943. The two most powerful battleships in the world were inactive during both the Guadalcanal and Solomons campaigns. (Naval History and Heritage Command)

14in. turrets and replacing them with a 230ft flight deck. The deck was not large enough to launch or recover aircraft, so two large catapults were also fitted. Once launched by catapult, the aircraft would recover on a conventional carrier or at a land base. A total of 22 aircraft could be carried on the flight deck and in the hangar below. The entire scheme was impractical and was not worth the resources spent to accomplish it. Neither ship ever launched an aircraft in combat. *Hyuga* underwent this modification between May and November 1943, and *Ise* was out of service from February to August 1943. After this conversion, both ships retained a main battery of eight 14in. guns.

Prior to the arrival of the Yamato class, the heart of the IJN's battle line was the two ships of the Nagato class. Commissioned in November 1920, they were the first Japanese ships to mount 16in. guns. Though modernized before the outbreak of World War II, they possessed inferior protection to contemporary USN battleships. However, they did have a much greater maximum speed, which made them marginally suitable for operations with carrier forces. Despite their considerable capabilities, neither saw action during the period covered by this book. *Mutsu* was destroyed in a magazine explosion in 1943.

Occupying a mythical place in the IJN's psyche was *Yamato* and its sister ship *Musashi*. Once freed from treaty restrictions, the Japanese decided to build battleships of immense proportions, with the intent of creating a ship so powerful in terms of protection, firepower, and propulsion that it would gain a qualitative overmatch against any USN battleship either in service or likely to enter service. The cost of creating such a ship was extremely expensive, only two of the envisaged four ships being completed.

Yamato joined the Combined Fleet just after the opening of the war; *Musashi* was commissioned in August 1942. Both ships spent the great majority of the period from August 1942 to November 1943 swinging at anchor in Truk lagoon; neither saw action during this time. Both did stints as Combined Fleet flagship. With their immense scale of protection, good top speed, and unparalleled firepower, they would have been difficult for the USN to handle had they been committed to the waters off Guadalcanal.

Heavy Cruisers

The IJN's heavy cruisers were very active during the first phase of the war. Despite their heavy operational tempo, only one had been lost in six months. This was *Mikuma* at Midway; its sister ship, *Mogami*, was heavily damaged in the same operation. While repairing *Mogami*, the Japanese took the opportunity to convert it into an aircraft-carrying cruiser with the capability of embarking 11 floatplanes.

Heavy cruisers were an important component of the Combined Fleet's night-fighting doctrine. Most of these ships were homogeneous in their capabilities. They were designed with a high-speed capability and a heavy armament of between six and ten 8in. guns. Despite the potential dangers of carrying huge, unprotected torpedo warheads, Japanese heavy cruisers were also fitted with a heavy torpedo battery. All IJN heavy cruisers also carried reloads for their torpedo tubes and floatplanes for scouting and to assist in night fighting.

JAPANESE HEAVY CRUISERS, JULY 1942–NOVEMBER 1943			
Available July 1942	Sunk July 1942–November 1943	New construction	In service November 1943
17	3	0	14

Oldest among the Combined Fleet's heavy cruisers were the virtually identical Furutaka and Aoba classes. Because they were designed before the Washington Naval Treaty came into effect, they were the smallest Japanese heavy cruisers, and with their smaller main and torpedo batteries, the least effective. They displaced less than the treaty's 10,000-ton limit, the only IJN heavy cruisers to do so. This made them less well protected than the heavier ships designed under treaty limitations. The four ships of these two classes were very similar. *Furutaka*, *Kako*, *Aoba*, and *Kinugasa* were commissioned in 1926 and 1927, and all were modernized before the war.

The first heavy cruisers designed under treaty restrictions were the four ships of the Myoko class. Though the original design adhered to the 10,000-ton limit, after the Naval General Staff had completed adding more weapons, the design was well overweight. This practice displayed a willful disregard for treaty restrictions and became commonplace in succeeding classes. The four ships in service were *Myoko*, *Nachi*, *Ashigara*, and *Haguro*.

Next up was the Takao class, commissioned in 1932, which was a slight improvement of the Myoko class. Ships in the class included *Takao*, *Atago*, *Maya*, and *Chokai*. All had been modernized before the war, but *Chokai* had been employed as a flagship and had not been as thoroughly modernized as its sister ships. At the start of the Guadalcanal campaign, *Chokai* was serving as the Eighth Fleet's flagship and was stationed at Rabaul.

The next two classes of Japanese heavy cruisers were originally designed as light cruisers. However, both had the capability to be upgraded from a main battery of 6.1in. to the standard heavy cruiser 8in. gun battery. As designed, the Mogami

Kako, pictured in 1940 during exercises, was a member of the 6th Cruiser Division and played a leading role in the Japanese victory at Savo Island. On its way back to Kavieng, it was torpedoed and sunk by USN submarine *S-44*, becoming the second Combined Fleet heavy cruiser lost during the war. (Naval History and Heritage Command)

Sendai was lead ship of the IJN's last class of 5,500-ton light cruisers. As can be seen from this prewar photograph of the cruiser on exercises, it was lightly armed. Among its many missions off Guadalcanal was participation in the second battle of Guadalcanal, in which it was undamaged. From January to May 1943, *Sendai* was very active in the Solomons. After a refit in Japan, it returned to the front but was sunk on November 1 at the battle of Empress Augusta Bay. (Yamato Museum)

class came in severely overweight and suffered from stability issues after the Japanese tried to cram in their customary heavy cruiser main gun and torpedo batteries on a 9,500-ton hull. After extensive modifications, the result was the most powerful class of heavy cruisers in the Combined Fleet. The four ships in the class were *Mogami*, *Mikuma*, *Suzuya*, and *Kumano*.

The final class of IJN heavy cruisers was much different since it emphasized aviation capabilities. The Tone class (consisting of *Tone* and *Chikuma*) was based on the design of the Mogami class and had provisions to be up-gunned with 8in. guns after Japan withdrew from the naval treaties. Only eight 8in. guns were carried, all fitted in turrets forward of the superstructure, leaving the entire stern area for aircraft facilities with space for five (as opposed to the usual three on other IJN heavy cruisers) floatplanes. Because of this enhanced aviation capability, both ships were almost always part of the Striking Force.

Light Cruisers

The IJN had a much different design priority for its light cruisers compared to the USN. Unlike American light cruisers, which were originally designed as scouts and then as well-protected gun platforms, the primary purpose of IJN light cruisers was to act as flagships for destroyer squadrons. As such, they possessed light gun and torpedo batteries and were weakly protected. They did offer facilities for an embarked destroyer division commander but were in no way comparable to the fighting power of modern USN light cruisers. As mentioned above, the IJN begin to build heavily armed and protected light cruisers comparable to USN ships, but since the Japanese preferred the hitting power and range of the larger 8in. gun, these were all converted to heavy cruisers.

The Combined Fleet began the war with 17 light cruisers and three cruiser-sized training ships. None were lost in the initial phase of the war. Fourteen of them were a standard 5,500-ton design optimized to act as destroyer squadron flagships. The final three light cruisers were second-line units. The three training cruisers were spacious by IJN standards and were used as flagships.

JAPANESE LIGHT CRUISERS, JULY 1942–NOVEMBER 1943			
Available July 1942	Sunk July 1942–November 1943	New construction	In service November 1943
20	4	4	20

The cruiser *Agano* moored at Truk sometime during 1943. The first of this class of four light cruisers was commissioned in October 1942. Despite its graceful appearance, *Agano* was not much of an improvement over the 5,500-ton cruisers. After arriving at Truk in December 1942, it conducted missions off New Guinea and Guadalcanal. After taking part in the battle of Empress Augusta Bay, it was torpedoed and sunk in February 1944 trying to return to Truk from Rabaul. (Yamato Museum)

The oldest IJN light cruisers were the two units of the Tenryu class laid down in 1917. At the start of the war, they were second-line units since they were slower and less well armed than the destroyers they were intended to lead. However, both were very active during the Guadalcanal and Solomons campaigns. After the failure of the Tenryu class, the Japanese increased the displacement of their next three classes of light cruisers to 5,500 tons (this was normal displacement – an IJN measure different from standard displacement used in treaty calculations). Larger ships could incorporate increases in speed and firepower, and the Japanese were happy with the results. The first 5,500-ton ships were the five ships of the Kuma class.

Seven ships of the Nagara class followed. They were virtual repeats of the Kuma class but had a larger bridge. The final 5,500-ton units were the three ships of the Sendai class. Again, they were virtual repeats of the previous class, but had a fourth stack, making them easy to recognize. Being the most modern of the 5,500-ton light cruisers, *Sendai*, *Jintsu*, and *Naka* were among the most active Combined Fleet light cruisers during the Guadalcanal and Solomons campaigns. *Jintsu* and *Naka*, along with Nagara-class unit *Abukuma*, were modified to operate Type 93 torpedoes before the war, so were heavily employed as destroyer squadron flagships.

In 1940, the IJN laid down a new class of light cruisers to replace the 5,500-ton ships. The Agano class of four ships was a graceful design but had limited capabilities while retaining the mission of leading destroyer squadrons. They did possess increases in firepower, especially in their torpedo battery, but were still under-armed compared to USN light cruisers. Two ships of this class were introduced into service between October 1942 and June 1943. The final light cruiser to entire service during the period of this book was a ship designed to act as the flagship of a submarine squadron. By the time it was commissioned in February 1943, the role for which it was designed no longer existed. With no mission, *Oyodo* was a white elephant and saw little service until being converted into the Combined Fleet's flagship in March 1944.

Destroyers

It is not an exaggeration to state that destroyers were the Combined Fleet's most important ships during the Guadalcanal and Solomons campaigns. IJN destroyers were designed as torpedo platforms and were a critical component in Japanese night-fighting doctrine. While they were superb torpedo platforms, they were indifferent antisubmarine platforms. A critical weakness was their lack of antiaircraft protection; at the start of the campaign, most Japanese destroyers carried only a pair of twin 25mm guns, which themselves were inferior weapons for the purpose for which they were designed. The result was that the Combined Fleet's destroyers were increasingly vulnerable to American airpower in the second half of 1942, and even more so during 1943. Of the 44 Japanese destroyers lost between August 1, 1942 and November 30, 1944, most were lost to air attack.

All the surface battles during the Guadalcanal and Solomons campaigns were fought at night. Except for Savo Island, Combined Fleet destroyers were the only Japanese ships present or which played a major role in the battles. When the Combined Fleet was forced into force preservation mode during the Solomons campaign, its destroyers were viewed as the most survivable and most expendable type of ship, leading to a very high operating tempo by an increasingly small force. The versatility of the Combined Fleet's destroyers was evinced when they were used in a transport role at Guadalcanal, New Guinea, and the Solomons. Overall, the Combined Fleet's destroyers proved very successful as surface combatants and transports during most of the period covered in this book, until late in 1943 when the IJN lost its edge in night fighting. However, Combined Fleet destroyer losses were very heavy.

JAPANESE DESTROYERS, JULY 1942–NOVEMBER 1943			
Available July 1942	Sunk July 1942–November 1943	New construction	In service November 1943
98	44	16	70

Of the 98 IJN destroyers available at the start of the Guadalcanal campaign, 21 were obsolescent Minekaze or Kamikaze classes and were not used in front-line roles. The Mutski class, though it dated from 1925, was used during the campaign and into 1943, though mainly in transport roles. This left 67 modern destroyers to cover all IJN requirements at the start of the Guadalcanal campaign. Not all were available to participate in operations, due to there being other areas of concern (the Aleutians and convoy escort), the constant toll of losses, and ships being unavailable during refits. Total new construction of destroyers entering service during the period was 16. These were high-quality ships, but their size and complexity made them unsuited for mass production, which is what the IJN needed at this point in the war.

The first modern Japanese destroyers were the 24 Special Type (or Fubuki and Akatsuki classes) destroyers, which entered service beginning in 1928. These were groundbreaking ships in their day, with a high maximum speed and impressive armament of nine 24in. torpedo tubes (with nine reloads) and main battery of six 5in. guns. One was lost in a collision in 1933 and two were lost early in the war, leaving 21 by the start of the Guadalcanal campaign.

Mutsuki-class destroyer *Mikasuki* was a veteran of the battles of Kula Gulf and Kolombangara. On July 28, it was caught by USAAF B-25 bombers off Cape Gloucester, New Britain, and sunk. Combined Fleet destroyers were increasingly vulnerable to air attacks as the campaign progressed. (Naval History and Heritage Command)

The London Naval Treaty of 1930 had a serious impact on IJN destroyer construction because of the IJN's overall tonnage restrictions and the restrictions placed on the size of individual ships. As a result, the next two groups, the Hatsuharu and Shiratsuyu classes, were smaller designs. By trying to jam too much on a small hull, the Hatsuharu class suffered from severe stability problems, but after modification still possessed five 5in. guns and six torpedo tubes. The Shiratsuyu class was the first to carry quadruple torpedo mounts.

By 1935, the IJN had decided to ignore the London Naval Treaty, which did not actually expire until the end of 1936. Doing so allowed the Japanese to return to building large destroyers with the size and capabilities of the Special Type units. The resulting Asashio, Kagero, and Yugumo classes were the heart of the Combined Fleet's wartime destroyer force. All possessed high speed, a six-gun main battery, and eight torpedo tubes in two quadruple mounts with eight reload torpedoes. The Yugumo class represented the ultimate refinement of the Special Type destroyer concept. The lead ship was commissioned in December 1941; ten were delivered between August 1942 and November 1943.

Totally impracticable was a single experimental ship named *Shimakaze*. While impressive on paper, with an extremely high top speed and an immense torpedo battery, such a complex design was impossible to build in sufficient numbers to have an impact, forcing the 16 additional ships planned for this class to be cancelled.

The Asashio class marked the return to large destroyers similar in capabilities to the Special Type ships. *Asashio* saw no action during the Guadalcanal campaign but was employed in March 1943 to escort a large convoy from Rabaul to Lae. It was sunk with all hands. (Yamato Museum)

Probably the best-balanced IJN destroyer was the Akizuki class, originally designed as an antiaircraft screening ship for carriers. On a large hull, Japanese designers mounted four twin turrets with the new and excellent 3.9in. gun and a quadruple torpedo mount. Their size also made them suited as flagships. During the period covered by this book, five more units were completed to join the lead ship already in service at the start of the Guadalcanal campaign.

The declining state of their destroyer force was a major concern for the Japanese. Destroyer losses were one of the reasons given for concluding the Guadalcanal campaign. In late December 1942, the Combined Fleet chief of staff lamented the perilous state of the destroyer force. The Eighth Fleet in Rabaul had only ten destroyers available. At Truk, the Second Fleet had only eight and the Third Fleet 12.

Submarines

The Combined Fleet's submarine force was largely ineffective during the first six months of the war. Intended to support the prewar decisive battle concept, several types of large submarines were designed with high speed, long range, and the firepower necessary to attack the USN's main fleet forces in support of Combined Fleet operations. Commerce attack was carried out during the initial period of the war, but was a decidedly secondary mission. After opening the Guadalcanal campaign with 51 boats, this overall number was unchanged for the next 16 months as losses and the retirement of older boats for training duties matched new production. Combined Fleet submarines enjoyed their period of greatest success during the Guadalcanal campaign, since they were able to operate in areas routinely transited by USN units. However, by the last half of 1943, the effectiveness of the IJN's submarine force declined significantly due to a lack of numbers, competing missions (such as being employed as transports), and increasingly active and effective Allied antisubmarine capabilities.

JAPANESE SUBMARINES, JULY 1942–NOVEMBER 1943			
Available July 1942	Sunk July 1942–November 1943	New construction	In service November 1943
51	33	47	65

TECHNICAL FACTORS

The IJN was on the cutting edge of naval technology when the war began. Amplifying this advantage was a highly trained and skilled cadre of sailors and airmen. On a small-unit basis, the ships and aircraft of the Combined Fleet were the best trained in the world.

Gunnery

The IJN devoted considerable resources and training time to master the intricacies of gunnery. After their victory over the Russians in 1905, the

Japanese took away the lesson that battles are won by big guns (such as those mounted on capital ships). A natural outgrowth of the belief in the primacy of big guns was a focus on outranging the enemy. If this could be achieved, heavy blows could be rained on the enemy before he could respond. This required extensive training in long-range tactics and the development of state-of-the-art fire control systems. By the start of the war, the IJN believed it had achieved the means to outrange the USN, with long-range gunnery placed at the center of daylight tactics. Both battleship and heavy cruiser gunnery focused on outranging tactics.

The final IJN class of fleet destroyers was the Akizuki class. One of the first ships in the class was photographed by American aircraft in the Solomons in 1943. This view shows the ship's four twin 3.9in. guns and a single quadruple bank of torpedo tubes. (Naval History and Heritage Command)

IJN guns were reliable and comparable in quality to their foreign counterparts. To gain the range required for outranging tactics, the Japanese relied on generating high muzzle velocities. Of the 12 battleships operational during the period, eight carried 14in. guns. Only two battleships carried 16in. weapons, with the two Yamato-class ships mounting 18.1in. guns – the largest ever fitted on a battleship. Each battleship also carried a secondary battery to engage targets at intermediate range. Since the Japanese did not develop a suitable dual-purpose gun, battleships also had to carry separate guns for long-range antiaircraft protection. All 18 heavy cruisers carried 8in. guns, which possessed excellent range but were handicapped by excessive salvo dispersion. Heavy cruiser secondary batteries comprised dual-purpose antiaircraft guns. Modern Japanese destroyers all carried a reliable long-range 5in. gun, but it was not comparable to its USN counterparts, being incapable of effective antiaircraft fire and hampered by a slow rate of fire.

PRINCIPAL IJN GUNS				
Type	Ships	Muzzle velocity (feet per second)	Shell weight (pounds)	Maximum range (yards)
14in./45 41st Year Type (1908)	Kongo, Fuso, Ise classes	2,543	1,485	38,770
16.1in./45 3rd Year Type (1914)	Nagato class	2,575	2,249	42,000
18.1in./45 Type 94	Yamato class	2,575	3,219	45,960
8in./50 Type 3 Model C/D	Aoba, Myoko classes	2,756	277	31,606
8in./50 Type 3 Model E	All other heavy cruisers	2,756	277	32,153
6in./50 41st Year Type (1908)	Kongo, Fuso classes	2,805	100	22,970
6.1in./60 3rd Year Type (1914)	Yamato class	3,035	123	29,960
5.5in./50 3rd Year Type (1914)	Ise, Nagato classes, all light cruisers	2,805	84	21,600 (depending on elevation)
5in./50 3rd Year Type (1914)	Destroyers	2,986–3,002	51	20,100

IJN fire control systems were comparable to those in service with foreign navies at the start of the war. However, Japanese fire control directors were bulky and relied excessively on manual inputs, but they had the advantage of excellent

This is a prewar photograph of *Takao*. Three ships of this very powerful class were available at Truk, but they saw little action during the campaign. *Takao* and *Atago* fought in the first naval battle of Guadalcanal but failed to complete their mission of bombarding Henderson Field. (Yamato Museum)

optics. In August 1942, only a handful of Japanese ships possessed radar. These early devices were only capable of performing air search. At no point during the period from August 1942 to November 1943 did the IJN develop and field a device capable of performing radar-guided gunnery. The lack of radar was a critical weakness.

Even with the IJN's emphasis on conducting gunnery at extended ranges, long-range gunnery is intrinsically difficult; the results during the first phase of the war were universally poor. Several examples highlight this. At the battle of the Java Sea in February 1942, the Japanese fought most of the battle at long range, as called for by their existing doctrine. In the daylight phases of the battle, conditions were as good as possible for long-range gunnery attacks. Even so, the results were poor. Of 1,619 8in. rounds fired from two heavy cruisers, only five found their target. Two days later, on March 1, during another day action fought at long range, two other heavy cruisers fired 1,171 8in. shells at a British heavy cruiser and scored just two hits. In the same action, an American destroyer was undamaged during the initial gunnery phase of the battle, and would have escaped if Japanese aircraft had not intervened.

Also on March 1, the Striking Force came across a USN destroyer. For 30 minutes, the battleship *Hiei* and heavy cruisers *Tone* and *Chikuma* fired at the fleeing destroyer at long range, with little success. Dive-bombers had to be called in to slow it down, after which it was sunk by gunfire. The two cruisers fired 844 8in. and 62 5in. rounds, with *Hiei* firing 210 14in. and 70 6in. and fellow battleship *Kirishima* 87 14in. and 62 6in. shells. This was an exorbitant expenditure of shells against a single destroyer.

Accuracy at reduced ranges was much better. On March 2, heavy cruisers *Atago* and *Takao* came across another USN destroyer and engaged it at night, with illumination provided by star shells, from about 6,000yds. After expending only 166 8in. rounds, the destroyer was sunk.

Antiaircraft Weapons

At the start of the war, Combined Fleet ships were inadequately armed to defend against air attack. This was due to two factors – mediocre weapons and inadequate numbers of these weapons. Because the Combined Fleet was rarely

The Kongo class was heavily used during the Guadalcanal campaign. This is *Kongo* pictured before the war. *Kongo* and sister ship *Haruna* conducted the Combined Fleet's most successful battleship action of the entire war when they bombarded Henderson Field on the night of October 13–14. (Yamato Museum)

exposed to air attack during the first six months of the war, this weakness was not revealed. Over the six months of the Guadalcanal campaign, it became apparent that Japanese ships were vulnerable to air attack. In 1942, IJN surface ships were fitted with few antiaircraft weapons. The saving grace for Japanese ships in the period was that hitting a moving ship is extremely difficult, especially if the ship is moving at speed and employing adept evasive maneuvers. Only in 1943 did the Combined Fleet start to augment the antiaircraft batteries on its warships, but this was only done incrementally.

The standard Japanese long-range antiaircraft weapon was the Type 89 5in./50 high-angle dual-purpose twin-gun mount. Because of its weight, it was only mounted on cruisers, battleships, and carriers. It was a decent weapon except for its relatively short maximum range. The Type 89 was handicapped by its dedicated fire control directors, which were unable to handle high-speed targets. Probably because of this, the standard IJN doctrine for its use was as a barrage weapon instead of more effective aimed fire against specific targets.

Every Combined Fleet combatant carried some number of light antiaircraft weapons for short-range protection. The vast majority were fitted with the Type 96 25mm gun, which came in twin and triple mounts (later a single mount was developed). Several problems reduced the effectiveness of the Type 96 as a short-range antiaircraft weapon. Among these were low training and elevating speeds, excessive muzzle blast, and a low rate of fire since the crew had to reload 15-round magazines. Some ships were fitted with a dedicated fire control director for the Type 96, but this was also unable to cope with fast targets. Those ships not fitted with the Type 96 carried only 13mm machine guns; these had too short a range to be effective and were mounted in grossly inadequate numbers.

PRINCIPAL IJN ANTIAIRCRAFT GUNS				
Type	Ships	Muzzle velocity (feet per second)	Rate of fire (per minute)	Effective range (yards)
5in./40 Type 89	Carriers, battleships, heavy cruisers	2,362	14 (maximum)	8,092
4.7in./45 Type 10	Some carriers and heavy cruisers	2,706	10–11 (maximum)	9,241
25mm Type 96	Almost all	2,952	110–120 (actual)	766–1,633

Torpedoes

Although Japanese naval guns were not outstanding, Japanese torpedoes were world-class. Japanese excellence in torpedoes was epitomized by the Type 93, with its unparalleled performance specifications. To give its destroyers a weapon capable of executing powerful night attacks without suffering crippling losses, the IJN started development on a wakeless torpedo capable of long ranges. To meet these requirements, the key was to develop an oxygen-propelled torpedo. The IJN persevered with this technology where other navies failed, and by 1936 the Type 93 entered service. With its long range and huge warhead, the Type 93 was treated by the IJN as a secret war-winning weapon. Not only did the Type 93 allow the IJN to outrange its enemies, but its huge warhead could sink any ship it hit. Torpedo tactics became the centerpiece of the IJN's night-fighting doctrine. Combined Fleet destroyers and light and heavy cruisers carried torpedoes, usually with a spare torpedo for each tube. With the help of high-speed reloading equipment, a well-drilled crew could reload their tubes in 15 minutes or less.

Combined Fleet submarines could not carry the huge Type 93, but they did carry another oxygen-propelled torpedo – the Type 95. Unlike USN submarine torpedoes, the Type 95 proved very reliable in service. Combined Fleet aircraft were also equipped with reliable air-launched torpedoes. The Type 91 could be dropped from altitudes up to 660ft and at speeds up to 120 knots. It possessed a relatively short range but had the high speed the Japanese preferred for close-in attacks.

PRINCIPAL IJN TORPEDOES			
Type	Platform	Warhead (in pounds)	Range (in yards)
Type 93 Model 1 Mod 2	Cruisers and destroyers	1,082	43,746 at 36 kts 35,000 at 40 kts 21,873 at 48 kts
Type 95	Most submarines	891	13,100 at 45–47 kts 9,850 at 49–51 kts
Type 91 Mod 2	Aircraft	452	2,200 at 41–43 kts

Japanese torpedo performance was mixed during the first six months of the war. At the battle of the Java Sea, the Combined Fleet employed its doctrine of firing the Type 93 at long range. Results were disappointing – of 153 Type 93s fired, only three hit a target. But the three that did hit each sank a Dutch ship, including two light cruisers. Given the ineffectiveness of Japanese long-range gunnery, these were the decisive blows of the battle. However, dozens of Type 93s exploded prematurely during this battle. In the engagement with the Allied force on March 1, another 25 Type 93s were fired and only a single hit was recorded. After fine-tuning, the Japanese still expected the Type 93 to be a decisive weapon.

The combination of the Type 97 carrier attack plane and the Type 91 torpedo gave the Combined Fleet a ship-killing capability unmatched by the USN.

Japanese torpedoes were effective at Pearl Harbor, accounting for three battleships. At Coral Sea and Midway, an American carrier was hit by two Type 91s at each battle, and on each occasion later sank.

Aircraft

Even after its defeat at Midway, where it lost four fleet carriers, the Combined Fleet still possessed a large carrier force. Every carrier had its own air group. Fleet carriers operated three squadrons – one each of fighters, dive-bombers (carrier bombers in IJN parlance), and torpedo planes (called carrier attack planes by the Japanese). Light carriers embarked a much smaller air group, composed of a fighter unit and a carrier attack plane unit.

The Combined Fleet's possession of a modern torpedo plane and a viable air-launched torpedo gave it a valuable edge in carrier battles. In the three battles where an American carrier was torpedoed, it eventually was lost. This was the fate of the *Hornet* at Santa Cruz. This is a Type 97 carrier attack plane taking off from *Shokaku* during the Pearl Harbor attack. (Naval History and Heritage Command)

The most numerous attack aircraft on Japanese carriers was the Nakajima B5N2 Navy Type 97 Carrier Attack Bomber Model 12. It was a versatile aircraft, with the ability to conduct torpedo attack missions or level bombing missions against land or naval targets. With its fairly high speed and reliable torpedo, it was the most capable torpedo bomber of the period. However, during the first two carrier battles of the war, its weaknesses were exposed. Unless escorted by fighters, it was vulnerable to interception by American fighters, as it carried only a single rear-firing machine gun for self-defense. Most importantly, it was very susceptible to damage since it lacked protection for its fuel tank or crew.

Fleet carriers carried the Aichi D3A1 Navy Type 99 Carrier Bomber Model 11. The Type 99 was a very accurate dive-bomber, as was proven on multiple occasions during the first six months of the war. Dive-bombers were viewed by the Japanese as less vulnerable than carrier attack aircraft, which had to approach their target at low altitude. Despite its many successes, the Type 99 was a mediocre aircraft, with a slow maximum speed and an ability to carry only a small payload. As with the Type 97 carrier attack plane, the Type 99 carrier bomber was unprotected and thus vulnerable to battle damage.

One of the outstanding weapons of the Combined Fleet was its standard carrier fighter. This was the Mitsubishi A6M2 Navy Type 0 Carrier Fighter Model 21 (called the Zero by the Americans and referred to as such in this book). At the start of the war, each fleet carrier embarked a squadron of 18 Zeros. After the first two carrier battles, this was increased to 27 fighters. With these fighters, Japanese carrier commanders had to cover offensive escort and fleet defense requirements. Several factors made the Zero an outstanding fighter – long range, fairly high speed, good firepower for the period, and supreme maneuverability. The Zero was also used by land-based units.

PRINCIPAL IJN AIRCRAFT IN DECEMBER 1941				
Type	Role	Maximum speed (knots)	Range (nm)	Payload
B5N2 Type 97	Torpedo and level bomber	235	1,240	1 Type 91 torpedo or 1,746lb of bombs
D3A1 Type 99	Dive-bomber	240	915	1 551lb and 2 132lb bombs
A6M2 Type 0	Air superiority/air defense	336	1,160	2 20mm cannons, 2 7.7mm machine guns
G3M2 Type 96	Land-based bomber	232	2,730	1 Type 91 torpedo or 1,746lb of bombs
G4M1 Type 1	Land-based bomber	266	3,750	1 Type 91 torpedo or 1,764lb of bombs

In addition to its large carrier-based air force, the Combined Fleet operated a significant land-based air force. Organized into flotillas, its principal aircraft included Zero fighters, long-range strike aircraft, and two types of flying boats for long-range reconnaissance. At the start of the war, the standard IJN long-range maritime strike aircraft was the Mitsubishi G3M2 Navy Type 96 Attack Bomber Model 22. It was successful in service, being capable of conducting torpedo or bombing attacks of land and naval targets. However, the aircraft's lack of defensive armament and protection was a weakness. By August 1942, the Type 96 was being replaced by the even longer-ranged Mitsubishi G4M1 Navy Type 1 Attack Bomber Model 11. Although this bomber possessed an impressive range, this was achieved at the expense of protection, with no armor or fuel tank protection making it potentially very vulnerable to enemy fighters.

The power of the Combined Fleet's land-based flotillas was a surprise to the Allies at the start of the war. On December 10, 1941, 85 land-based bombers sank the Royal Navy battleship *Prince of Wales* and the battlecruiser *Repulse* in the South China Sea with a combination of torpedo and bomb attacks. Such a feat had never before been accomplished. Although unable to replicate this success later in the Dutch East Indies (DEI) campaign, land-based bombers did conduct attacks on the Allied Striking Force on February 4 and 15. While no ships were hit, on both occasions the Allied force aborted its mission.

Against land targets, the Combined Fleet's land-based bomber force also proved itself to be formidable if escorted by friendly fighters. IJN land-based air power played the leading role in gaining air superiority over the Philippines, and then proceeded to assist Imperial Japanese Army air force units in gaining air superiority over Malaya and the DEI.

The standard Japanese dive-bomber during the Guadalcanal and Solomons campaigns was the Type 99 carrier bomber. It flew off carriers and operated from land bases, as shown in this view. Though an accurate dive-bomber, the Type 99 needed fighter escort to be effective. (Imperial Japanese Navy, now in the Public Domain)

HOW THE FLEET OPERATED

DOCTRINE AND COMMAND

The Commander of the Combined Fleet since August 1939 was Admiral Yamamoto Isoroku. He has gone down in history as a great admiral, but this reputation is completely undeserved. The bedrock of his greatness was the Combined Fleet's string of victories at the start of the war. However, Pearl Harbor was a strategic blunder, and the attack did not render significant operational or tactical rewards. The Combined Fleet's early successes were gained against unprepared and outnumbered Allied forces. Beginning in May 1942, against forces of roughly equal strength, the Combined Fleet suffered a string of disasters and defeats. The last was at Guadalcanal, where Yamamoto failed to recognize the importance of the battle and therefore did not use all the resources at his disposal. Yamamoto was killed on April 18, 1943, in an aircraft shot down over Bougainville after the failure of his last offensive, Operation *I*.

Replacing Yamamoto was not easy, since he was revered and even worshipped by his staff and was seen by the entire Combined Fleet as a gifted and inspirational leader. Before his death, Yamamoto selected Admiral Koga Mineichi as his successor. Koga, who became full admiral in May 1942, gets little scrutiny since he served as commander in chief of the Combined Fleet for less than a year and fought no major battles during his tenure. Nevertheless, in the short time he was in command he put his stamp on the Combined Fleet and in some ways was a more forward-thinking leader than Yamamoto.

Koga was a firm advocate of the IJN's fixation on fighting a "decisive battle." In Koga's mind, the decisive battle had to be fought in 1943, when the Combined Fleet still had a 50 percent chance of victory. Koga hated mounting a passive defense, so he started to come up with a plan to fight a decisive battle. The plan, dubbed the *Z* Operation, was the basis for the Combined Fleet's effort to defend the Marianas in June 1944.

Combined Fleet Organization

At the start of the Pacific War, the Combined Fleet leveraged its peacetime organization to create task-organized forces for the various missions required to achieve the First Operational Phase objectives. Following its defeat at Midway, a large reorganization was necessary, but vestiges of the Combined Fleet's peacetime structure remained.

To defend the newly conquered DEI, the Southwest Area Fleet was activated on April 10, 1942. Under it were the First, Second, and Third Southern Expeditionary Fleets, all established on the same day. These fleets were responsible for garrisoning Japan's Southeast Asian holdings and for conducting operations in the Indian Ocean.

Operations in the South Pacific were the responsibility of the Southeast Area Fleet, formed on December 24, 1942. Under its direct control as of December 24 were the Eleventh Air Fleet, composed of land-based air flotillas, and the Eighth Fleet. The Eighth Fleet was previously established on July 14, and the Eleventh Air Fleet dated from before the war. Both were based at Rabaul and were responsible for the daily operations of the Guadalcanal and Solomons campaigns.

In addition to the area fleet commands, the prewar standing fleets survived. Traditionally, these were formed on a functional basis and were available for operations anywhere in the Pacific. The First Fleet was traditionally the Combined Fleet's battle line, and therefore was viewed as its premier force. With the role of the battleships much diminished, the First Fleet became a backwater command and was eventually deactivated on February 25, 1944. It held virtually no operational units during the Guadalcanal and Solomons campaigns. The 2nd Battleship Division was assigned the two Fuso-class battleships and the two Nagato-class units. *Ise* and *Hyuga* were detached from the First Fleet and placed under Combined Fleet control during their conversions. The 1st Battleship Division, with the two Yamato-class ships, was treated as a special case and was directly subordinate to the Combined Fleet. On July 14, the day of the Combined Fleet's reorganization, the 3rd Battleship Division (with the four Kongo-class units) was placed under Second and Third Fleet control.

The 6th Cruiser Division, with the four oldest heavy cruisers in the IJN, was nominally assigned to the First Fleet but was actually under Eighth Fleet control. The 9th Cruiser Division, with the IJN's two torpedo cruisers, remained under First Fleet control until December 1942, when the two ships were assigned to the Combined Fleet for conversion. The 1st and 3rd Destroyer Squadrons were also under First Fleet control at the start of the Guadalcanal campaign. As destroyer losses mounted, the various subordinate divisions were siphoned off to other commands until no destroyers remained in the First Fleet by early 1943. On April 1, the 11th

Admiral Yamamoto Isoroku was Commander of the Combined Fleet from the start of the Pacific War until his death in April 1943. This is his official portrait from 1943. His performance during the Guadalcanal campaign was halfhearted and the series of under-resourced attempts Yamamoto orchestrated to retake the island were all defeated. (Naval History and Heritage Command)

Destroyer Squadron was established and placed under the First Fleet. This unit controlled newly constructed destroyers after commissioning. Once their sea trials were completed, the ships were assigned to front-line destroyer divisions.

The Second Fleet was the IJN's traditional scouting fleet and the home fleet for most of its heavy cruisers. As part of the July 14 reorganization, many of its cruisers were reassigned to other formations. The 4th Cruiser Division remained with the four Atago-class units. However, *Chokai* was assigned to the Eighth Fleet from July 14 until August 20, 1943. Half of the 5th Cruiser Division, *Haguro* and *Myoko*, also remained. The 7th Cruiser Division with the two remaining Mogami-class units, the 8th Cruiser Division with the two Tone-class units, and *Kongo* and *Haruna* from the 3rd Battleship Division, were all transferred to the Third Fleet on July 14. Two destroyer squadrons were also attached – the 2nd, with flagship *Jintsu* and three destroyer divisions, and the 4th, with flagship *Yura* and three destroyer divisions.

The biggest change in the July 14, 1942 reorganization was the reactivation of the Third Fleet and its transformation into the Combined Fleet's carrier force. The 1st and 2nd Carrier Divisions were destroyed at Midway. On July 14, they were reestablished and assigned to the Third Fleet. In the new 1st Carrier Division were the two Shokaku-class fleet carriers and light carrier *Zuiho*, while the 2nd Carrier Division comprised the two Junyo-class carriers and *Ryujo*. Newly constructed light carrier *Ryuho* was assigned to the 2nd Carrier Division on June 12, 1943.

A major premise of the reorganization was to augment the escort force of the carriers. The 7th Cruiser Division was assigned with *Kumano* and *Suzuya*, and was later augmented with *Mogami* on June 10, 1943. Also assigned was the 8th Cruiser Division. *Hiei* and *Kirishima* of the new 11th Battleship Division were also assigned to the new Third Fleet; when these were lost in November, *Kongo* and *Haruna* of the 3rd Battleship Division were moved over to take their place. The elite 10th Destroyer Squadron provided the screen for the heavy ships, with flagship *Nagara* (later the new *Agano* in November 1942) and five destroyer divisions with the Combined Fleet's newest destroyers.

The Fourth, or Mandate, Fleet had responsibility for a huge geographic area, including the Gilberts, Marshalls, and the Carolines. It had no major units other than the light cruiser *Kashima* and the 14th Cruiser Division of two light cruisers, added on April 1, 1943. Its primary assets were four base forces with an array of local defense units, including gunboats, minesweepers, submarine chasers, and a large collection of ground units to garrison the many islands in its area of responsibility.

The Fifth Fleet was responsible for operations in the Aleutians and the defense of the northern approaches to Japan. At the start of the war, it was a backwater command, but this changed when the Japanese seized two islands in the Aleutians and had to periodically resupply them and eventually withdraw the garrison from one of them. Its primary asset was the 21st Cruiser Division, with heavy cruiser *Nachi* and light cruisers *Tama* and *Kiso*. The subordinate 22nd Picket Boat Squadron was assigned many converted merchant ships to provide early warning

Admiral Koga Mineichi took over the Combined Fleet in April 1943 and remained in this post until his death the following year. He oversaw a defensive strategy during the Solomons campaign. His plans for a decisive battle with the USN in 1943 went unrealized. (Naval History and Heritage Command)

if an American task force approached northern Japan. On April 1, 1943, the 1st Destroyer Squadron was assigned the flagship *Abukuma* and two destroyer divisions. On July 29, 1943, this force skillfully evacuated the Japanese garrison from Kiska Island without the Americans even being aware.

The Sixth Fleet was the Combined Fleet's primary submarine command, but its strength fluctuated as submarine divisions were assigned to other fleets for specific duties and older boats were retired and sent to Japan for training duties. By November 1943, the strength of the fleet was only about 18 boats. Fleet headquarters was on light cruiser *Katori*, anchored at Kwajalein Atoll in the Marshalls. The 1st Submarine Squadron was subordinate throughout this period, and by the end of 1943 had two subordinate submarine divisions. The 3rd Submarine Squadron also was assigned two subordinate divisions for most of the period. The fleet's final submarine squadron was the 8th, also with two submarine divisions. Each of the squadrons was assigned a submarine tender, and the 3rd and 8th Submarine Squadrons were also assigned a large submarine designed to act as a deployed flagship.

Based at Rabaul, the Combined Fleet's newest fleet was the 8th. It had few assets formally assigned to it, but was constantly being reinforced from other fleets because Combined Fleet forces operating out of Rabaul were in constant contact with the enemy and suffered losses accordingly. Among the units constantly assigned to it were the 18th Cruiser Squadron, with the IJN's two oldest light cruisers, and the 3rd Destroyer Squadron, with flagship *Sendai* in late February 1943. A squadron of short-ranged submarines was also assigned. Most of the units of the fleet were from its five subordinate base forces (1st, 2nd, 7th, 8th, and 14th), with the usual array of light naval forces and ground units for defense of the various islands and installations in the Eighth Fleet's area of responsibility. Since the Eighth Fleet was on the front line, it had many Special Naval Landing Force, construction, and antiaircraft units assigned to it.

Koga reshaped the Combined Fleet to fight his decisive battle. In August 1943, he formed integrated carrier task groups along the lines of the USN's Fast Carrier Task Force. One carrier group was built around the Third Fleet. One of the Third Fleet's carrier divisions was transferred to the Second Fleet and became the basis for a second carrier group. These two task groups formed the Mobile Fleet and were placed under the command of the Third Fleet, the IJN's carrier command. Koga also created a land-based air fleet to work directly with the Mobile Fleet in the projected decisive battle.

During 1943, Koga sought battle with the USN's carrier fleet in the Central Pacific. Between September 18 and 25, the Combined Fleet's carrier force moved to Eniwetok in the Marshall Islands in response to an American carrier raid in the Gilberts. The following month, Koga repeated the exercise with a larger force from October 17–26, when an American carrier force raided Wake Island. In both cases, no contact was made with the American fleet. Even if it had been detected, Koga probably would have declined to seek an engagement because the conditions for a successful outcome did not exist.

As the Guadalcanal campaign opened, the Combined Fleet flagship was *Yamato*. On February 12, 1943, the flag shifted to *Musashi*. Both ships sat at anchor in Truk Atoll during the Guadalcanal and Solomons campaigns, thereby gaining the reputation as being luxurious hotels for the embarked staff. It would have been more appropriate for the Combined Fleet's staff to move its headquarters ashore, where it could have communicated freely.

Doctrine

During the years leading up to the Pacific War, the IJN's belief in the decisive battle concept grew, undiminished by reality. Against an industrialized nation like the United States, there was no possibility that a single battle would decide the entire war. However, the Japanese needed a scheme to create the illusion of potential victory against a much more powerful opponent, and the decisive battle strategy provided a potential path to victory.

On the tactical level, each component of the Combined Fleet had a role to play in the carefully choreographed decisive battle. To perfect their roles, the Combined Fleet trained hard during its annual training program. Of course, there was no climactic battle between massed fleets in the Pacific War of the nature the Combined Fleet trained so hard for. While some of the decisive battle tactics and training did not translate into the actual Pacific War, some parts proved very useful.

One part that did not translate at all was an emphasis on a clash between battle lines conducted at long range during daylight. All the surface actions during the Guadalcanal and Solomons campaigns took place at night. Fortunately for the Combined Fleet, night combat was an integral part of the decisive battle design. When the war came, the Japanese enjoyed an immediate advantage in night combat by virtue of their superior training, tactics, equipment, and weaponry.

Japanese night-fighting tactics focused on the capabilities of the long-range Type 93 torpedo. Following a "long-distance concealed firing" by heavy cruisers, destroyer squadrons would close with and complete the destruction of the enemy. Executing this scheme required constant practice, including elemental training by the various ships themselves on the actual loading, aiming, and firing of the Type 93, but also the skills required maneuvering formations of ships together to properly employ massed torpedo tactics.

In addition to the training required for night fighting, the Japanese placed great emphasis on developing the tools required. An area of particular importance was optical devices. Among these were powerful binoculars with sophisticated magnification and light-gathering capabilities. These varied in size up to 8in., with the Type 88 Model 1 introduced in 1932 being especially effective. The higher the quality of the lens and the bigger its size, the more effective it was in low-light conditions. The success of these devices was shown by the fact that they were often more effective than early American radars at night. The Japanese also developed star shells, including a parachute-suspended type in 1935. Japanese guns also used smokeless powder to avoid disclosing the location of the firing ship.

Jintsu was damaged by an aircraft bomb on August 25, 1942, and was forced to return to Japan, and thus missed the rest of the Guadalcanal campaign. At the battle of Kolombangara on July 13, 1943, it was the target of a barrage from three USN light cruisers. After going dead in the water, *Jintsu* was hit by a destroyer-launched torpedo and sank with heavy loss of life. (Yamato Museum)

Myoko was the lead ship of the IJN's first class of Treaty cruisers. These powerful and well-protected ships proved to be formidable opponents during the war. Only two ships in the class took part in the Guadalcanal and Solomons campaigns, with a capstone appearance at the battle of Empress Augusta Bay. (Naval History and Heritage Command)

The Japanese emphasis on small-unit tactics translated directly to night engagements in the Guadalcanal and Solomons campaigns. Cruisers and destroyers were trained to approach the target at high speed, with the flagship as the guide unit. Targets were deconflicted so that there was no over-concentration on a single target. Each ship would fire a complete torpedo salvo. The surprise torpedo attack was exploited with a close-quarters attack using gunfire. Following the example of the flagship, each ship would use searchlights to illuminate the enemy. Heavy cruisers were expected to use their main batteries to engage enemy targets at the longest range possible.

Doctrine was useful as a general guide for night combat, but Japanese commanders modified it during the campaign. The Japanese were fully aware that the Americans were using radar. Not wanting to be surprised, the Japanese modified their tactics later in the campaign to fire their torpedoes as soon as they gained contact on the enemy and could get a fire control solution. Following that, the Japanese would move out of range to reload torpedoes and then seek to re-engage. Gunfire was not favored, but was used immediately if surprised.

At the start of the war, the Combined Fleet's carrier force was dominant. Following Midway, the Japanese were forced to rebuild their carrier force. They examined the reasons for their defeat and made significant changes in their carrier tactics. As part of the Combined Fleet's July 14 reorganization, the First Air Fleet became the Third Fleet, which was now clearly established as the Combined Fleet's primary offensive force. The Second Fleet was to be used as an advanced screen for the carriers. Ideally, this force would be deployed well ahead of the carriers, where they would be in position to finish off any American ships crippled by air attack and to absorb some of the American air attacks intended for the Japanese carriers.

The composition of the air groups of the fleet carriers were changed in light of the Midway experience. The fighter squadron was increased to 27 aircraft, as was the dive-bomber squadron. The torpedo plane squadron was reduced to 18 aircraft, reflecting the Japanese belief that these aircraft were more vulnerable.

The Japanese carrier force changed its tactics after Midway. Scouting was emphasized and provided with sufficient resources, even if this meant reduction of the striking power of the carriers. The fleet carriers were seen as offensive platforms, while the light carriers were to be used primarily as a provider of fighters for fleet air defense. During the first two carrier battles of the war, Japanese doctrine featured attacking heavily defended naval targets simultaneously with dive- and torpedo bombers to overwhelm the defenses and minimize losses to the more vulnerable torpedo bombers. Going into the Guadalcanal campaign, the Japanese decided to hold their torpedo planes in reserve until the dive-bombers crippled the American carriers. This tactic was used unsuccessfully at Eastern Solomons; by Santa Cruz, the Japanese returned to their traditional combined-arms attack with simultaneous dive-and torpedo bomber attacks.

The Japanese carrier force's salient weakness demonstrated at Midway was a lack of air defense capabilities. This was primarily due to a glaring lack of early warning. To compensate for this, *Shokaku* was equipped with radar before the battle of the Eastern Solomons. The Japanese used radar with some success at Santa Cruz; combined with the use of the Advance Force, which acted as an air defense picket, this greatly diminished the likelihood that Japanese carriers would be totally surprised as at Midway.

Combined Fleet submarine employment doctrine was focused on direct support to the battle fleet at the expense of attacking enemy commerce. Accordingly, the most modern submarines were used to support major Combined Fleet operations. With rare exceptions, this proved to be a failure. In the Guadalcanal campaign, the Combined Fleet persisted with its prewar doctrine for the use of submarines. The primary reason for the failure of this doctrine was the inability of the Japanese to get their submarines where USN main fleet units were operating. This problem was solved for them at Guadalcanal when the Americans insisted on operating in the same area. As a result, Japanese submarines had a rich haul, sinking one American carrier, damaging another and forcing it out of action for months, and damaging a modern battleship, among other successes. At no other time during the war did the Combined Fleet's submarine force have such an impact. On the other hand, efforts by Japanese submarines to attack American supply lines to Guadalcanal ended in failure. The desperate supply situation of Japanese troops on Guadalcanal forced the Combined Fleet to begin using submarines for resupply missions in December. Dispersion of effort was a key factor in the ultimate failure of the IJN's submarine force.

INTELLIGENCE, COMMUNICATION AND DECEPTION

The problems with IJN intelligence efforts were thoroughly addressed in *Japanese Combined Fleet 1941–42*. Without belaboring the background for the weakness of the Combined Fleet in the intelligence arena, the key reasons were a lack of resources devoted to this highly technical craft and a general disdain on the Combined Fleet staff for the importance of intelligence. Instead of allowing intelligence to drive operations, as it should, Combined Fleet operations personnel were only comfortable with intelligence if it didn't clash with plans and operations already underway.

The experiences of the Combined Fleet's intelligence officer illustrate this point. There was a single intelligence officer on the Combined Fleet staff, and he also served as the communications officer. At the start of the Guadalcanal

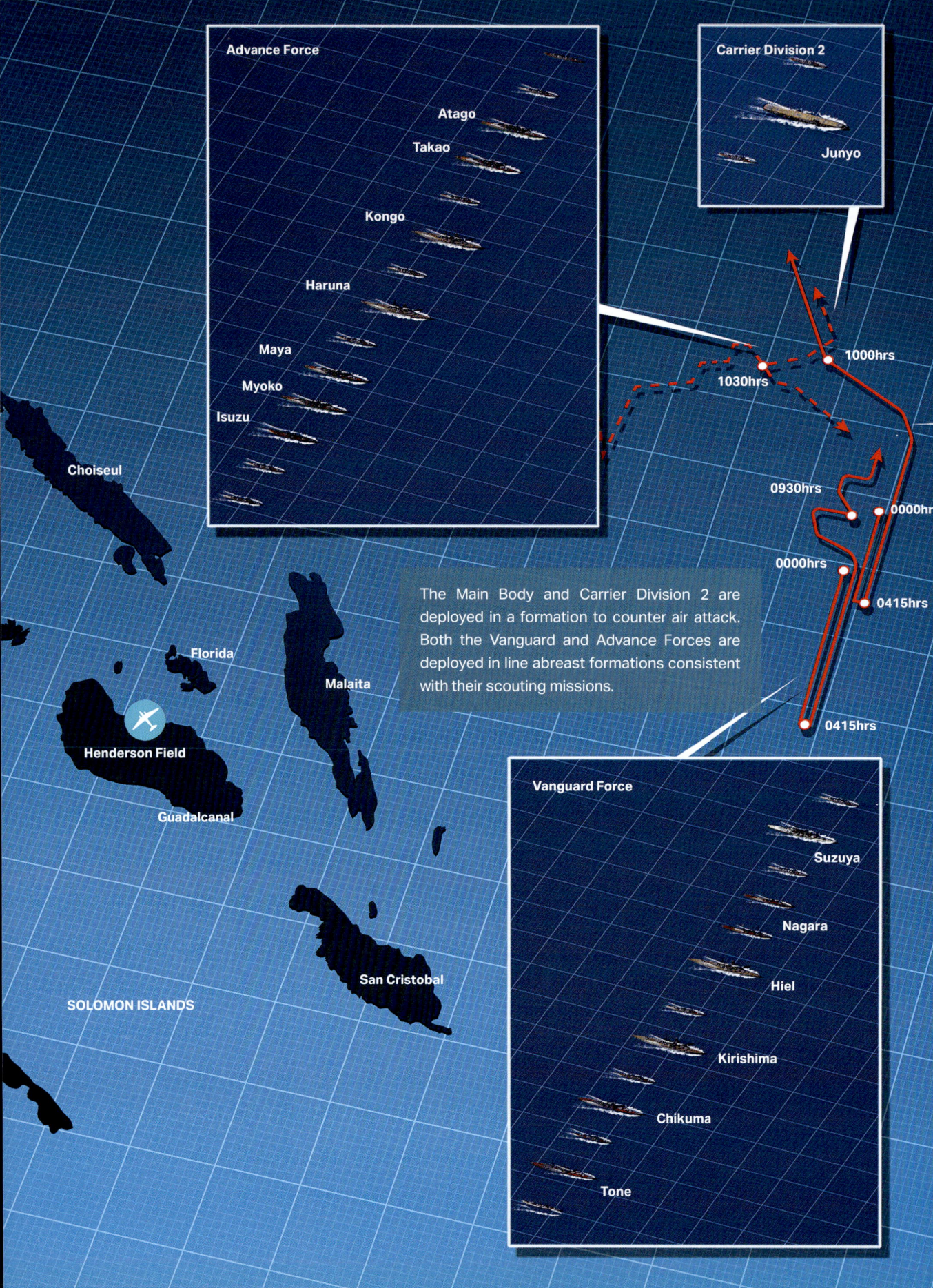

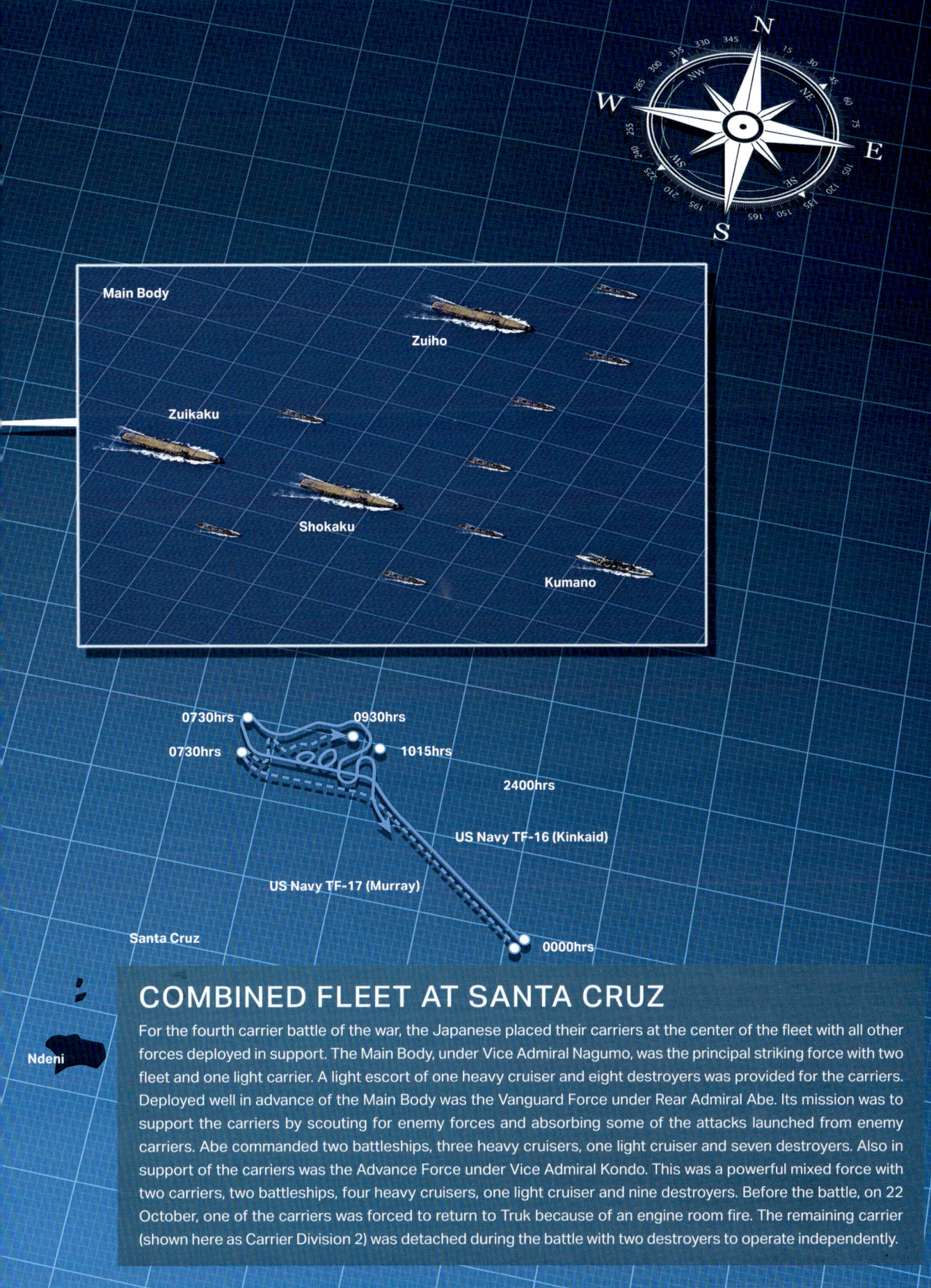

COMBINED FLEET AT SANTA CRUZ

For the fourth carrier battle of the war, the Japanese placed their carriers at the center of the fleet with all other forces deployed in support. The Main Body, under Vice Admiral Nagumo, was the principal striking force with two fleet and one light carrier. A light escort of one heavy cruiser and eight destroyers was provided for the carriers. Deployed well in advance of the Main Body was the Vanguard Force under Rear Admiral Abe. Its mission was to support the carriers by scouting for enemy forces and absorbing some of the attacks launched from enemy carriers. Abe commanded two battleships, three heavy cruisers, one light cruiser and seven destroyers. Also in support of the carriers was the Advance Force under Vice Admiral Kondo. This was a powerful mixed force with two carriers, two battleships, four heavy cruisers, one light cruiser and nine destroyers. Before the battle, on 22 October, one of the carriers was forced to return to Truk because of an engine room fire. The remaining carrier (shown here as Carrier Division 2) was detached during the battle with two destroyers to operate independently.

campaign this was Commander Wada Yushiro. After Yamamoto's death in April 1943, he was replaced as part of a general staff turnover by Commander Nakajima Chikataka. Upon his arrival, he found that aside from a small radio intelligence unit under his direct control, composed of three officers and six enlisted personnel, he was the only officer on the entire staff performing any intelligence work. Soon, this took up most of his time, at the expense of his communications duties.

Nakajima's intelligence duties were not well defined, nor was the procedure used to inject intelligence into the planning process. He produced no daily intelligence summary or any regular intelligence summary of any kind. He did not maintain any sort of situation plot of enemy forces. There was no order-of-battle reference available on American forces, since all this information was kept in his head. Furthermore, there was no coordination with subordinate fleets because there were no meetings between the Combined Fleet intelligence officer and the intelligence officers of the other fleets. There was no rigor put into his assessments. In Nakajima's own words, as new information arrived, "I would think it over and come to some conclusion. It was not a very scientific method."

Good intelligence analysis requires good intelligence sources. The IJN lacked this vital ingredient. The Japanese were heavily reliant on air searches for information on American naval movements. Indeed, they were too reliant on this source. Though daily searches were flown, most out of the seaplane base at Rekata Bay on Santa Isebel Island north of Guadalcanal, if these failed to find anything the Japanese were virtually blind. Often, if the flying boat crews found something, their poor ship recognition skills undermined the usefulness of their reporting. Japanese aircrews did not use photography as a matter of course, probably because there were no specialized photo interpreters to analyze the photography. Nakajima noted that there were no photo interpreters assigned to the Combined Fleet staff.

The IJN's standard fighter during the period was the Type 0 (Zero), which served in both carrier and land-based units. This view shows a group of Zeros preparing for a mission from Rabaul. The Type 0 was unable to gain air superiority over Guadalcanal since it was flying at extreme range from Rabaul and because of the relatively few fighters available. (Imperial Japanese Navy, now in the Public Domain)

Other sources included the use of aircraft launched from large submarines to surveil Allied naval facilities in the region. In October and November, E14Y aircraft overflew Espiritu Santo, Noumea, Efate, and Fiji. This slow aircraft was very vulnerable to interception, so these flights usually took place during the early morning. The information gained was of marginal utility. Much more useful was the information provided by a gunnery officer from *Yamato* posted as an observer with long-range optical equipment atop Mount Austen on Guadalcanal. From this position, he overlooked both the airfields and Ironbottom Sound. His reports were generally accurate and were provided in near real time.

The IJN did not have success penetrating USN codes, primarily due to lack of resources. However, it did gain valuable operational intelligence by performing traffic analysis. By correlating the call signs of USN naval units and then determining how often they communicated and at what message precedence, the Japanese could determine the likelihood of large-scale USN operations. If the transmission could be geo-located using high-frequency direction finding (HF/DF, or "huff duff"), this would be even more valuable.

Analysis of American radio traffic was performed by specialized units. The 8th Communications Unit located at Rabaul and the 4th Communications Unit in the Mandates had the collateral mission to monitor USN communications. The most capable unit in this regard was the 1st Combined Communications Unit stationed at Rabaul, which possessed special duty personnel trained in cryptanalysis and operated an HF/DF station.

Using all the sources available in combination with a weak analysis protocol of the raw data collected did not result in useful intelligence being provided to Combined Fleet commanders. For example, analysis of the externals of USN radio communications could be taken as an indicator of heightened USN activity, but it did not provide the specificity to make it actionable and was not a reliable method to discern American intentions. The first real indicator of an American operation underway was usually when a sighting report was provided by a reconnaissance aircraft.

Not surprisingly, this resulted in a string of intelligence failures, the most salient of which will be discussed here. When the Americans launched their assault on Guadalcanal, it caught the Japanese totally by surprise. So complete was this surprise that seven large Japanese flying boats were destroyed by strafing American fighters. The largest American fleet of the war to date was able to steam into Japanese-controlled waters and seize an important installation that the Japanese must have known was vulnerable. As a result, the Combined Fleet was only able to respond with local forces based at nearby Rabaul. Without knowing the strength of the American forces off Guadalcanal or the location of the American carriers, Vice-Admiral Mikawa launched an attack with an inferior force. As detailed below, although this rush to combat ended in a major Japanese victory, this was only because of an avalanche of Allied errors.

Japanese planning throughout the campaign registered between foolhardy and merely negligent. The primary reason for this was a willful disregard for intelligence. The best example of this was a consistent Japanese underestimation of the size of the American garrison on Guadalcanal, which resulted in a series of piecemeal attacks that had little hope of success.

Upon learning of the American landing, the Army and Navy Sections of the Imperial General Headquarters both believed that the invasion was nothing more than a "reconnaissance in force." The Japanese should have known better,

Fubuki was the lead ship of the Special Type class of destroyers. When completed in 1928, it was the most powerful destroyer in the world. *Fubuki* conducted 11 transport or sweep missions off Guadalcanal before being sunk by cruiser gunfire at the battle of Cape Esperance on October 11, 1942. (Yamato Museum)

since on August 7 their aircraft reported 30 transports present off the island, indicative of a major operation. By August 10, the Imperial Navy was sure that a division was ashore on Guadalcanal. Within days of arriving at this accurate assessment, the estimate of the size of the American force on Guadalcanal was dramatically revised downward. Thus began a pattern of bending intelligence to preconceived notions of American intentions and capabilities which set up a cycle of piecemeal commitment. As a result, bad intelligence combined with overconfidence and a desire to dislodge the Marines as quickly as possible led to a decision to attack with a single battalion. The attack failed completely as the actual size of the Marine garrison on Guadalcanal was some 10,000 men. The same pattern was evinced in September when the IJA believed that a reinforced brigade would suffice to expel an entrenched Marine division. Not surprisingly, this attack also ended in failure.

The battle of Cape Esperance was an example of how weak or no operational intelligence on USN naval movements influenced operations. After Savo Island, the Combined Fleet controlled the nighttime waters around the island. The Japanese used the cover of darkness to run countless destroyers to the island loaded with IJA personnel, confident that the USN would not intervene. At some point this had to end, and when it did so on the night of October 11–12, the Japanese surface force was surprised and defeated.

The carrier battle of Santa Cruz provides another problem in Japanese intelligence, namely an inability to perform basic order-of-battle intelligence. By October 1942, the fate of the few American carriers in service since the start of the war should have been easy to ascertain. No new fleet carriers had been commissioned, so only the six carriers known to have been in the Pacific during 1942 should have been considered. In fact, the USN was down to two operational carriers in October 1942, and both were at Santa Cruz. The Japanese rightly claimed a major victory in this carrier clash but exaggerated the scope of the victory, initially claiming four USN carriers sunk before settling on three. The difference between the claimed victories and the actual number of carriers even available for service was explained by the Japanese granting the Americans new production. At this point, the IJN had lost track of the basic USN carrier order of battle. *Enterprise* was not sunk at Santa Cruz, and was repaired enough to make an appearance in mid-November when the Americans committed everything they had to defeat Yamamoto's November offensive.

Prior to the second naval battle of Guadalcanal, Japanese reconnaissance aircraft continually misidentified the American surface force south of Guadalcanal as two cruisers and two destroyers. The American force actually comprised two modern battleships and four destroyers – a critical difference. Perhaps because of this, Yamamoto declined to make a maximum effort to bombard Henderson Field, even though he had two additional battleships and several heavy cruisers available. On the night of November 15, the two misidentified battleships repelled the final Japanese offensive of the campaign.

Another indication of the poor state of IJN intelligence is provided by the failure of the Japanese to foresee the first American move into the Central Solomons. The Japanese believed that their April air offensive had seriously delayed any American offensive. Though New Georgia was the obvious target because it contained the critical airfield at Munda, the actual landing on June 30 on nearby Rendova Island was a total surprise to the Japanese. The first indication that an American invasion was underway was when a submarine spotted the invasion force at midnight on June 29 on its way to Rendova. Failure to foresee the invasion meant that the Japanese did not stage sufficient air or naval forces to Rabaul. Thus, the USN was able to mount a major amphibious operation within easy striking range of Rabaul.

This view of the battle of Kula Gulf demonstrates the ease with which Japanese destroyer crews located their targets. In the foreground is the light cruiser *Helena* firing its 6in. battery; astern of it is the light cruiser *St Louis*. Within minutes of this photograph being taken, Type 93s struck *Helena*. (Naval History and Heritage Command)

When the Americans invaded Bougainville in November, the Japanese were once again caught by surprise. Some 60,000 IJA and IJN troops were on the island, most in the southern part of the island, which was seen as the most likely area for an American landing. Instead, the Americans landed in Empress Augusta Bay, where only 2,000–3,000 Japanese troops were located. Though the Japanese were aware that an American invasion of Bougainville was in the offing, both the timing and the location of the landing were unknown. The result was that the Americans established a beachhead large enough to build three airfields within 200nm of Rabaul.

If having a weak ability to produce usable intelligence wasn't bad enough, the IJN was catastrophically poor in communications security. American operations to stop Japanese offensives at Coral Sea and Midway were directly linked to the IJN's inability to protect its own codes. After Midway, IJN communications security improved. On October 1, the Combined Fleet instituted a call sign and code change. This was only a temporary setback for American cryptanalysts, who were able to recover call signs and penetrate the principal IJN code known as JN-25 to the degree that they correctly predicted Yamamoto's October offensive. USN intelligence analysts also correctly predicted the Japanese November

THE COMBINED FLEET, 1 AUGUST, 1942

offensive. Early warning of these major Japanese operations provided American commanders with the time to move their slender assets to defeat both of them.

Most large Combined Fleet moves were known in advance by the Americans. Occasionally, the Americans had the capability to react with their own forces. An example was a planned large Japanese troop convoy from Rabaul to Lae on New Guinea. With the timetable of the operation revealed, the USAAF was able to conduct searches to find the convoy and cover the source of their advanced knowledge. On March 3, 1943, Allied air power overwhelmed the convoy and inflicted a major defeat on the Japanese in the battle of the Bismarck Sea, sinking all eight of the transports in the convoy and four of the eight escorting destroyers. An even more dramatic example of the failure of the Combined Fleet to guard its operational codes was provided by the American operation to assassinate Yamamoto as he conducted an inspection trip to the front. When the message containing Yamamoto's exact itinerary was intercepted and decoded, the Americans used it to shoot down his aircraft and kill the Combined Fleet's revered commander.

In yet another example of poor communications security, Admiral Koga's major decision to move the Second Fleet from Truk to Rabaul to attack the American beachhead on Bougainville was known to the USN ahead of time. The Americans did not have any heavy ships in the area to contend with such a force, but they did have a carrier task group available. The American commander used his foreknowledge of Koga's intentions to plan a carrier strike on the Second Fleet's heavy cruisers as soon as they arrived at Rabaul. The resulting attack damaged most of the cruisers and ended the threat to the Bougainville beachhead.

On other occasions, the Combined Fleet could turn the tables on the Americans. An example of such operational deception occurred at the end of the Guadalcanal campaign. To evacuate their garrison, the Japanese planned three runs by large groups of destroyers. Designated Operation *KE*, the operation was a complete success. The entire garrison was removed for the loss of a single destroyer. The operation was conducted immediately after an IJN code change which helped camouflage the evacuation, but the Combined Fleet's deception plan of making preparations for the evacuation look like renewed reinforcement operations proved totally convincing to American intelligence analysts. Ironically, the Americans fell prey to the temptation to assess the enemy's intentions and ignore his capabilities, just as the Japanese had done so often earlier in the campaign.

LOGISTICS AND FACILITIES

As the focus of the naval war in the Pacific shifted to the Solomons in August 1942 and remained there throughout 1943, the IJN was forced to conduct operations where it had few permanent naval facilities. The Japanese made use of two excellent

natural harbors to support their Solomons operations – Truk in the Central Pacific and Rabaul in the South Pacific. While both locations had multiple airfields, neither had been built up into a true naval base. Naval operations were supported from floating support assets stationed at these anchorages. This did not prove to be a huge detriment unless ships were damaged or required overhaul, in which case they had to return to naval facilities in Japan.

Much more of a factor on operations was the availability of bunker fuel in the forward areas. The critical factor here was the availability of tankers to move the fuel from the DEI and then to Truk or Rabaul. In addition to a tanker shortage, the IJN had an even more pronounced shortage of oilers equipped with the means to provide underway replenishment to units conducting extended operations.

Facilities in Japan

The Japanese Home Islands were broken down into four naval districts – Yokosuka, Kure, Maizuru, and Sasebo. Each naval district had a major shipyard capable of construction and repairs, making them the center of the IJN's logistical network. Each naval district included supply and fuel depots necessary to service the needs of the Combined Fleet. Ominato on the northern island of Hokkaido was the location of a fifth naval yard, but it was only used for major repair work. In addition to the naval districts, there were seven naval guard districts centered on minor bases. Two of these, the Pescadores in the Formosa Strait and Port Arthur in northern China, were deactivated in 1942. Complementing the naval yards were eight major commercial yards which were capable of construction, modernization, and repair of fleet units.

In addition to the facilities in the Home Islands, several former Allied naval facilities captured early in the war were put back into service by the Japanese. The most useful was the former Royal Navy Seletar Naval Base in Singapore. This facility possessed a well-developed infrastructure, including a large dry dock, and could perform overhauls of major units. Other useful facilities were the former Dutch naval base at Surabaya on the island of Java and the British naval base at Hong Kong.

IJN NAVAL SHIPYARDS OUTSIDE JAPAN		
Location	Date operational	Types of work performed
Shanghai, China	1938	Repairs of small combatants; merchant ship construction and repair
Hong Kong	December 1941	Repairs of combatants up to light cruiser size; merchant ship construction and repair
Singapore	February 1942	Repair and overhaul of any size IJN combatant
Surabaya, Java	March 1942	Repairs of small combatants and former Dutch naval and merchant ships
Cavite, Philippines	May 1942	Temporary repairs of combatants as large as heavy cruisers; repair of former American naval ships

The scale of losses and ships damaged during the first six months of the war were below Japanese expectations. This meant that Japanese shipyards were not swamped by requirements to perform battle repairs. However, ships needed regular refits, and except for Singapore, overhaul of major fleet units could only be done in Japan. Gradually, this and the mounting toll of damaged ships resulted in the Combined Fleet's prewar divisions and squadrons losing their coherence. By the time of the Solomons campaign, destroyer squadrons which had a prewar strength of 12–16 ships were operating with half that number.

Construction of new ships was not keeping up with losses, especially after the loss rate skyrocketed from August 1942 onwards. From August 1 until the end of 1943, a span of 17 months, Japanese shipyards and naval yards produced the following ships:

JAPANESE NAVAL CONSTRUCTION, AUGUST 1 1942–NOVEMBER 30 1943		
Ship type	Number	Classes
Carriers	4	Light carriers *Ryuho*, *Chiyoda*; escort carriers *Chuyo*, *Kaiyo*
Battleships	1	*Musashi*
Heavy cruisers	0	
Light cruisers	3	Agano – 2; Oyodo – 1
Destroyers	16	Yugumo – 10; Shimakaze – 1; Akizuki – 5
Submarines	47	Fleet submarines (21): Type B1 – 6; Type KD7 – 9; Type B2 – 5; Type C3 – 1. Medium submarines: Type K6 – 10. Coastal submarines: Type KS – 16
Escorts	15	Etorofu – 13; Mikura – 2

These numbers may seem respectable, but must be placed into context. In 1943 alone, the United States produced 65 carriers of all types, two battleships, 11 heavy and light cruisers, 128 destroyers, 298 escorts, and 55 submarines. Granted that some of these ships were destined for service in the Atlantic, it is readily apparent that Japanese shipbuilding capabilities were woefully inadequate. Japanese naval construction was unable to keep pace with losses. The only area in which the Combined Fleet had grown by the end of 1943 was in escorts. Though production of escorts began to ramp up in 1943, it was totally inadequate to meet the demands of protecting Japan's sea lines of communication. Construction of major fleet units (destroyers and larger) was also totally inadequate, which meant that the overall size of the Combined Fleet had decreased by the end of 1943. In the key area of carriers, the IJN was able to slightly increase its numbers, but only through the conversion of passenger ships and assorted fleet auxiliaries, which resulted in the delivery of second-rate carriers. During the period of this book's focus, the IJN did not receive a single purpose-built fleet carrier. Production of submarines was strong during the second half of 1942 and throughout 1943, but this was mainly attributable to a shift from the large prewar-designed fleet boats to a new class of medium submarines and a class of much smaller coastal defense submarines.

The same weakness was evident in Japanese production of merchant ships. Total tonnage of merchant ship construction in 1942 was 260,059, and in 1943 this figure grew to 769,085. This was insufficient to replace growing wartime losses and paled in comparison to American merchant production, which totaled almost

17 million tons over the same period. Tankers were the most critical component of Japan's merchant fleet. In December 1941, Japan possessed 49 merchant tankers and the IJN had nine dedicated fleet oilers – clearly too few to meet wartime demands. The IJN was forced to requisition 77 merchant tankers for conversion to auxiliary oilers. In late 1942, due to a shortage of tankers necessary to meet wartime demand for oil and gasoline, some cargo ships and ore carriers were converted to temporary tankers during their construction. Twenty existing passenger-cargo ships were also converted to emergency tankers.

Truk Atoll

The Combined Fleet's principal base from July 1942 until February 1944 was Truk Atoll in the Caroline Islands. The history and development of Truk is detailed in *Japanese Combined Fleet 1941–42*. Truk was geographically well situated to support the Combined Fleet's operations in the Solomons, but although the Japanese had occupied it since 1914, it had not been well developed as a naval base. Before the war, civilian facilities on Dublon Island were commandeered by the IJN and became the foundation of the Fourth Naval Dockyard, under the control of the Number 4 Naval Construction and Repair Department. The facility was not extensive, but it did include a 1,000-man workforce, a 30-ton floating crane, and 2,500-ton dry dock. The headquarters of the department was in the southeastern part of the island near Dublon Town and included 22 wooden buildings, including repair shops, warehouses, and barracks. In total, the shore installations could repair no more than two destroyer-sized ships (up to 2,000 tons) and five 600-ton ships at a time. Dublon Island also served as the main cargo-receiving area for the atoll's garrison, so had warehouses, a refrigeration building, and a two-story barracks. Most of the buildings were connected by a small-gauge railroad. A sawmill was built nearby. Wharf space was limited and there were no docking facilities for large ships, so a collection of barges, harbor craft, tugs, and sampans were used to load and unload ships, with the assistance of a derrick, carts, and trucks ashore.

Aside from its austere naval base, Truk boasted an array of other facilities. These included four airstrips, seaplanes bases, and a torpedo boat station; the 85th Submarine Base, established in May 1942, could perform minor repairs to submarines. There were five communication stations around the atoll, with the main one located on Dublon Island. A radio direction-finding station was also

After the battle of Kula Gulf, the destroyer *Nagatsuki* ran aground on Kolombangara Island on July 6. Later that day, the helpless destroyer was attacked by Allied aircraft and destroyed. *Nagatsuki* was a member of the Mutsuki class, six of which were modified as destroyer transports and used heavily during the Solomons campaign. (Naval History and Heritage Command)

built on the atoll and radar was present to give warning of approaching aircraft.

As the number of ships damaged in the South Pacific continued to grow in 1942 and throughout 1943, the IJN moved the bulk of its repair ships to Truk to handle the influx. The IJN's only design-built repair ship was the 10,500-ton *Akashi*, completed in 1940. It possessed impressive facilities to conduct and coordinate repairs – a fully equipped tool room, a blueprint room, an electric repair shop, and a machine shop equipped with 114 various machine tools capable of casting, forging, welding, copper working, and woodworking. *Akashi* was fitted with a 23-ton crane, two 10-ton cranes, and two 5-ton cranes to transfer repair parts and handle stores. The Japanese optimistically estimated that *Akashi* had the capability to conduct 40 percent of the repairs needed by the Combined Fleet. *Akashi* arrived at Truk in June 1942 and was based there throughout 1943. It soon became apparent other repair ships were needed to augment *Akashi*. At various times, *Shoei Maru*, *Urakami Maru*, *Hakkai Maru*, and *Yamashimo Maru* were active at Truk; these were four of the IJN's six converted repair ships.

Combined Fleet operations in the South Pacific were supported through Truk Atoll in the Central Pacific. Aircraft bound for Rabaul were staged through Truk's airfields, including Eten Island Airfield, shown here. In the background is Dublon Island, where most of the infrastructure at the atoll was built. (Naval History and Heritage Command)

As a major naval base, Truk needed the capability to store large amounts of bunker fuel. However, this was a problem because Dublon had only six fuel storage tanks, with a capacity of 49,000 tons. A single pier was equipped to handle the fuel, but it could not accommodate tankers, only fuel barges. There were only three such barges. One held 500 tons of fuel, the second 200 tons, and the third just 50 tons. Frequent resupply from tankers was necessary, and the process of fueling ships and refilling the storage tanks was slow since fuel had to be lightered using the fuel barges. The lack of fuel storage capacity to support the Combined Fleet required that precious tankers be kept at the atoll and used for storage, and that super-battleships *Yamato* and *Musashi* be used to store fuel for distribution to other fleet units.

Availability of fuel was a factor in Combined Fleet operations during the campaign, though to what degree this influenced operations is difficult to determine. What is clear is that large-scale fleet operations were an infrequent occurrence and that the majority of the IJN's fuel-guzzling battleships were not heavily employed. As discussed later, this was probably more due to the IJN's reluctance to employ its battleships in a non-decisive battle situation than it was to fuel considerations. Nevertheless, fuel was a constant issue. At the start of April 1942, the entire Japanese (not just IJN) heavy oil stock was 3,184,000 tons. From April 1942 to March 1943, the IJN burned 3,660,000 tons of fuel, a monthly average of 305,000 tons. Since demand exceeded existing stockpiles, the Japanese war economy was dependent on fuel production from Southeast Asia and the availability of tankers to move the fuel to where it was needed.

The majority of the IJN's daily average fuel consumption of some 10,000 tons per days was burned by the Combined Fleet, with only a portion devoted to operations in the Solomons. In the second half of 1942, the IJN's fuel situation was already serious. Fuel reserves at Kure, one of the most important bases, were down to 65,000 tons. In this context, mounting a large operation off Guadalcanal was a heavy burden, as even a destroyer steaming at its economical speed burned 30 tons of fuel per day and a Nagato-class battleship 150 tons per day. Fuel expenditure rates went up exponentially if ships were required to steam at full speed. The continual operation of destroyers running at high speed from the Shortlands anchorage south of Bougainville to Guadalcanal was a substantial drain on fuel stocks in Rabaul. To mount a major operation from Truk with heavy ships, lasting up to two weeks, carried an immense fuel cost. Depending on the number and type of ships and the duration of the operations, a single operation might require 15,000–25,000 tons of fuel. What might seem like a simple operation to move a force of battleships from Truk to bombard Henderson Field on Guadalcanal imposed a similarly high fuel cost.

Truk was also the funnel for getting aircraft to the South Pacific. Four airfields were built on the atoll between November 1941 and February 1944. The airfield on Eten Island had revetments, aircraft repair shops, and maintenance shops. Dublon served as a major maintenance installation for seaplanes. The 104th Air Arsenal was established at Truk as an assembly and repair organization. Typically, aircraft would be moved to Truk by ship; once unloaded and assembled, they would fly south to Rabaul.

Rabaul

The major base directly supporting IJN operations in the Solomons was Rabaul, on the Gazelle Peninsula on the northeastern tip of New Britain Island. Rabaul is blessed with one of the largest natural harbors in the Pacific. This was Simpson Harbor, which received its name from a Royal Navy explorer in 1872. The magnificent harbor measures 8 miles by 6 miles wide.

In 1910, the Germans moved the administrative center of their Bismarck Islands protectorate to Rabaul. Before World War I, they built a wharf and warehouse in the harbor area and an extensive surrounding road network. Early in World War I, Australian troops occupied Rabaul, and it became the capital of the Mandated Territory of New Guinea. By 1939, it held a population of some 10,000, boasting a civilian airfield at Lakunai and a military airfield at Vunakanau, located 9 miles south of the town. Severe volcanic eruptions in 1937, which blanketed the town in ash, convinced the Australians to move the capital to Lae on New Guinea, but this move was not complete by 1941.

Rabaul supported a complex of four large airfields, among them Vunakanau Airfield. In this view, a G4M medium bomber is being subjected to parafrag attack from a USAAF bomber. It must be remembered that throughout the Guadalcanal and Solomons campaigns, the airfields around Rabaul were under constant pressure from USAAF units. (NARA)

Rabaul was on the list of Japanese objectives for the first phase of the war. Originally, it was considered important to capture Rabaul to provide strategic depth for Truk. Later, as the Japanese began their second-phase expansion plans, Rabaul became the crucial base for operations in New Guinea and deeper into the South Pacific. So important did the Japanese consider Rabaul that four carriers of the Striking Force were employed to cover the invasion. On January 20 and 22, 1942, Nagumo's carriers launched large strikes against Rabaul, encountering feeble Australian resistance. IJA troops landed before dawn on January 23. The Australian garrison soon scattered, and the Japanese took over Rabaul and its facilities.

Harbor facilities at Rabaul were not well developed, as this view of small ships alongside the base's piers shows. In the foreground are parafrag bombs dropped by USAAF bombers. (NARA)

The Japanese developed Rabaul into their most important base in the South Pacific. By January 25, Lakunai was ready to receive fighters, and it could accommodate bombers the following month. Vunakanau became the primary Japanese airfield. To complement the two existing airfields, the Japanese completed Rapopo, 14 miles southeast of the town, in December 1942, Tobera (inland of Rapopo) in August 1943, and Keravat, 13 miles southwest of Rabaul. Keravat was situated in an area of poor drainage and was later abandoned. The other four airfields featured concrete runways and an extensive network of 80–120 revetments at each airfield, with a total of 265 revetments for fighters and 166 for bombers.

As airfield construction progressed, so did expansion of the facilities in the town itself. Rabaul tripled in size, with 600 new structures and an aggregate floor space of 2.8 million square feet. Twenty-three diesel power stations with a capacity of about a megawatt were built, and 13 new wells were drilled with a capacity of 290,000 gallons per day. New road construction totaled 395 miles.

However, Rabaul was poorly developed as a naval base. The Japanese did not construct any permanent facilities ashore to repair ships or store bunker fuel. The lack of a dry dock and of shipbuilding facilities meant that repair ships had to be brought in. These could accomplish minor to medium repairs, but major structural repairs had to be performed in Japan. The first repair ship to arrive was *Shoei Maru* in March 1942. Its tenure in the area was short-lived, as it was sunk by an American submarine in May that year. The expanding war in the Solomons forced the Japanese to get more serious about performing repairs at Rabaul. The 8th Naval Construction and Repair Department was established in September 1942. The following month, repair ship *Hakkai Maru* arrived at Rabaul; repair ship *Yamabiko Maru* followed in October. These ships were busy repairing several cruisers, destroyers, and auxiliaries; larger ships with battle damage were sent to Truk. *Yamabiko Maru* was badly damaged by bombs in November 1943, leaving Rabaul the next month after sending its repair equipment ashore. In February 1944, *Hakkai Maru* was sunk by an aircraft torpedo in Simpson Harbor.

COMBAT AND ANALYSIS

THE FLEET IN COMBAT

The longest naval campaign of the Pacific War began on August 7, 1942, when American Marines landed on Guadalcanal and other points in the Southern Solomons. Initially caught by surprise, Vice-Admiral Mikawa rounded up any Eighth Fleet ships available in the Rabaul area and launched a counterattack. Mikawa was confident that his scratch force could defeat the larger Allied force, given the Japanese edge in night-fighting tactics. Though spotted by Allied submarines and aircraft, the Japanese gained tactical surprise when they appeared in the waters between Guadalcanal and Savo Island in the early hours of August 9. Even the presence of radar on some American ships failed to give warning; on this occasion, Japanese night optics proved superior.

The battle occurred in two phases. In the first, Mikawa fell upon a group of two Allied heavy cruisers and two destroyers, shattering them in just seven minutes with torpedo and gun attacks. The Australian heavy cruiser *Canberra* was mortally damaged, and USN heavy cruiser *Chicago* was damaged by a torpedo. Since the Allied group failed to report it had been attacked, Mikawa was able to surprise a second USN group of three heavy cruisers and two destroyers. Using the same tactics of attacking first with torpedoes and then following up with gunfire, each of the heavy cruisers was struck by numerous shells at close range and two were hit by torpedoes. All three were mortally damaged.

BATTLE OF SAVO ISLAND, AUGUST 9 1942		
	Forces involved	Results
Allied	5 heavy cruisers, 6 destroyers	4 heavy cruisers sunk, 1 cruiser damaged, 1 destroyer damaged
Japanese	5 heavy cruisers, 2 light cruisers, 1 destroyer	Light damage to 5 cruisers

Critically, after crushing the Allied covering force, Mikawa failed to follow up his victory by attacking the 18 American transports present. IJN doctrine was

Following the American invasion of Guadalcanal, the Japanese struck back with G4M bombers from Rabaul. The attack on August 8 featured 27 G4Ms escorted by 15 Zeros. After failing to find the American carriers, they went after shipping located off Guadalcanal. This remarkable photograph shows three of the aircraft on their attack run. Of the 23 bombers that attacked, 18 were lost, making this by far the deadliest day of the campaign for the Combined Fleet's bomber force. Another attempt to attack shipping off Guadalcanal on November 12 also ended in very costly failure. (Naval History and Heritage Command)

focused on the destruction of enemy naval power – attacking transports was not a priority. In this case, had Mikawa attacked the transports it would have provided the foundation for the defeat of the first USN offensive in the Pacific War.

By mid-August, Yamamoto had readied a force to move into the South Pacific to deal with the American incursion in the Solomons. Since it was assumed that the ground offensive would retake the airfield, the Combined Fleet's mission was to destroy the American fleet. The Combined Fleet also planned to move a small convoy with 1,500 men to the island.

BATTLE OF THE EASTERN SOLOMONS, AUGUST 24 1942		
	Forces involved	Results
American	Fleet carriers *Saratoga* and *Enterprise*, 1 battleship, 4 heavy cruisers, 2 light cruisers, 13 destroyers	*Enterprise* lightly damaged, 25 aircraft lost
Japanese	Fleet carriers *Shokaku* and *Zuikaku*, light carrier *Ryujo*, 1 seaplane carrier, 2 battleships, 9 heavy cruisers, 2 light cruisers, 17 destroyers	*Ryujo* sunk, 1 destroyer sunk, 1 seaplane carrier damaged, 75 aircraft lost

The resulting battle, fought on August 24, was the third – and most indecisive – carrier battle of the war. To neutralize the airfield, Nagumo detached *Ryujo* and retained his two heavy carriers in preparation for when the American carriers were spotted. For the first time, the Japanese carriers led by Vice-Admiral Nagumo had adequate escorts in the form of Advance and Vanguard Forces. These were spotted by American search aircraft, as was the detached *Ryujo*, but Nagumo's fleet carriers were not. A floatplane from *Chikuma* spotted the American carriers and Nagumo launched a strike force totaling 73 aircraft. *Enterprise* was attacked by dive-bombers and struck by two bombs, but damage was only light. A second strike failed to locate the wounded *Enterprise*, which survived the battle. In the process, Japanese aircraft losses were heavy.

The American riposte was quick in coming but was largely ineffective. *Ryujo* was sunk by aircraft from *Saratoga*, but the attack against Nagumo's main force never found his carriers. Instead, the escorts were bombed, with seaplane carrier *Chitose* taking light damage. The following day, the reinforcement convoy

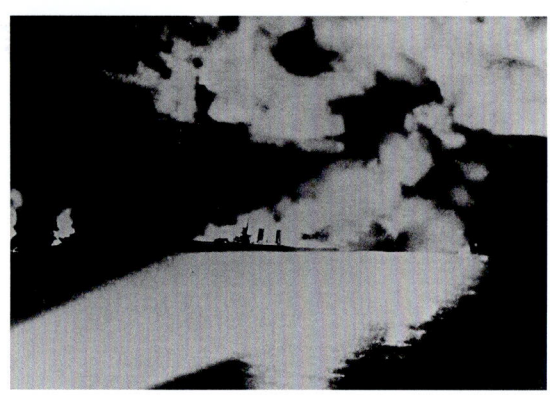

In the first surface action of the Guadalcanal campaign, the Combined Fleet gave convincing proof of its mastery of night combat. Four Allied heavy cruisers were sunk in a single night, with no Japanese ships lost. Photographed from a Japanese cruiser on August 9, 1942, this is American heavy cruiser *Quincy* burning and illuminated by Japanese searchlights. (Naval History and Heritage Command)

was attacked by American land-based aircraft. After a destroyer and a transport were sunk, Yamamoto ordered the operation cancelled.

After its defeat at Savo Island, the USN ceded the waters around Guadalcanal at night to the Japanese. As a result, the Combined Fleet was able to conduct regular destroyer runs to the island to build up the Japanese garrison on the island. On the night of October 11–12, the Japanese planned a major operation with two high-speed seaplane carriers delivering artillery to the island and a bombardment of the airfield by three heavy cruisers and two destroyers. No opposition was expected. When an American task force showed up to stop the bombardment, the Japanese commander was totally surprised. In addition, some of the USN ships had improved radar, which detected the approaching Japanese at 27,700yds. Though the American commander failed to fully exploit the warning, his force was able to fire first.

In the initial phase of the battle, USN gunnery mortally damaged heavy cruiser *Furutaka*, heavily damaged another cruiser, and sank a destroyer. In the second phase, heavy cruiser *Kinugasa* showed the individual excellence of Japanese ships and crews by heavily damaging an American light cruiser and damaging a heavy cruiser.

BATTLE OF CAPE ESPERANCE, OCTOBER 11–12 1942		
	Forces involved	Results
American	2 heavy cruisers, 2 light cruisers, 5 destroyers	1 light cruiser heavily damaged, 1 heavy cruiser damaged, 1 destroyer sunk, 1 destroyer damaged
Japanese	3 heavy cruisers, 2 destroyers	1 heavy cruiser sunk, 1 heavily damaged, 1 damaged; 1 destroyer sunk, 1 damaged

Cape Esperance was a convincing USN victory, but it did not change the fact that the Japanese still commanded the nighttime seas around Guadalcanal. On October 14, battleships *Kongo* and *Haruna* pulverized Henderson Field with 973 14in. shells. The temporary neutralization of the airfield allowed the Japanese to move a six-ship convoy to the island.

The culmination of Yamamoto's October offensive was a major fleet operation to defeat the USN after the IJA secured the airfield. The ground attack was postponed twice. When it was finally launched on the night of October 24, it failed. Unable to wait any longer, Yamamoto sent his fleet south on October 24. After a day of maneuvering on October 25, the Combined Fleet ordered Nagumo to close on the following day and attack the Americans.

On October 26, both carrier forces spotted each other off the Santa Cruz islands early in the morning. The resulting American strike was fragmented. Only a single dive-bomber squadron from *Hornet* found the Japanese carriers, but four 1,000lb bomb hits forced *Shokaku* out of the battle. The Japanese strike was the best-coordinated of the entire war. *Hornet* was the target of 53 Japanese aircraft and was crippled by two torpedo and three bomb hits. The second wave of 44 aircraft attacked *Enterprise* but enjoyed much less success. Two bomb hits were scored; critically, none of the 16 torpedo bombers were able to secure a hit, allowing *Enterprise* to escape.

In the final phase of the battle, *Junyo*'s strikes damaged the battleship *South Dakota* and a light cruiser. Further damage to *Hornet* precluded the carrier's escape, and its burning hulk was eventually sunk by Japanese destroyers. Santa Cruz was the only Japanese carrier battle victory of the war. Although sure they had scored a major victory, sinking three or even four American carriers, Yamamoto and his staff miscalculated its impact. With such losses, the American carrier force could no longer play a role in the campaign. In fact, *Enterprise*'s escape was critical, and it would play a crucial role in the following month. Nagumo lost no carriers, but aircraft losses were very high (99) and aircrew losses were crippling – 145, more than at Midway. The scale of these losses had short- and long-term implications for the Combined Fleet's carrier force.

BATTLE OF SANTA CRUZ, OCTOBER 26 1942

	Forces involved	Results
American	Fleet carriers *Enterprise* and *Hornet*, 1 battleship, 3 heavy cruisers, 3 light cruisers, 14 destroyers	*Hornet* sunk, *Enterprise* damaged, 1 battleship damaged, 1 light cruiser damaged, 1 destroyer sunk, 80 aircraft lost
Japanese	Fleet carriers *Shokaku*, *Zuikaku*, and *Junyo*, light carrier *Zuiho*, 4 battleships, 8 heavy cruisers, 2 light cruisers, 24 destroyers	*Shokaku* and *Zuiho* damaged, 1 heavy cruiser damaged, 99 aircraft lost

The Bombardment (overleaf)

In mid-October 1942, the Combined Fleet conducted one of its most effective operations of the entire war in the waters off Guadalcanal. A large surface force under the command of Rear Admiral Takeo Kurita entered Ironbottom Sound with the mission of dealing Henderson Field a knockout blow. Kurita led a force of the battleships *Kongo* and *Haruna*, with an escort of one light cruiser and nine destroyers. The Japanese had prepared this operation with care. *Kongo* carried special Type 3 incendiary shells for its 14in. shells. Accuracy would be ensured by a gunnery officer from *Yamato* stationed atop Mount Austen overlooking the airfield and by four spotter and illumination aircraft, one with *Kongo*'s gunnery officer aboard. The bombardment began at 0133hrs on October 14 from a range of 29,500yds. Both battleships fired salvo after salvo at the airfield, expending a total of 973 shells. Except for a brief respite at 0213hrs when the battleships made a turn, the bombardment proceeded unhindered until 0256hrs. Only in the last few minutes of the operation did four American PT boats make an appearance, which prompted Kurita to suspend the bombardment five minutes early. The result was the temporary neutralization of Henderson Field's offensive power, since virtually all the aviation fuel had been destroyed, only seven of 39 dive-bombers could still fly, and all the torpedo planes at the airfield were destroyed. In the aftermath of the bombardment, the Japanese were able to deliver some 4,500 men and a bounty of supplies and equipment to the island aboard a six-ship convoy. This scene shows the opening of the bombardment, with *Kongo* opening fire. In the background is *Haruna*, which had yet to begin its bombardment.

First Naval Battle of Guadalcanal

To move the required numbers of troops to Guadalcanal for the next ground assault to take Henderson Field, the Combined Fleet planned a repeat battleship bombardment of the airfield. With the airfield suppressed, a large convoy of 11 transports could reach the island. Though the Japanese commander of the bombardment force did not expect to encounter opposition, he was taking no chances and deployed a squadron of five destroyers in advance of his main force. When the Japanese encountered a large USN task group sent to stop the bombardment at all costs, the advance destroyers were out of position. The American commander had the benefit of early radar detection of the approaching Japanese, but he hesitated to act. What ensued was the most vicious night battle of the entire war. Twenty-seven ships engaged in close-quarters combat, from which only nine emerged unscathed.

In the confused action, Japanese (and American) gunfire, combined with a Japanese torpedo, inflicted mortal damage on American light cruiser *Atlanta*. Light cruiser *Juneau* was struck by a destroyer-launched torpedo and then sunk by a submarine attack while leaving the battle area. The final American light cruiser suffered only light damage. Both heavy cruisers were battered by Japanese gunfire and the American commander was killed on his flagship. The American destroyer force was shattered, with four ships sunk and two heavily damaged. Only two emerged from the action unscathed. Nevertheless, the exchange was far from one-sided. American ships bravely pressed their attacks, concentrating on lead battleship *Hiei*, which was hit by a storm of fire – 28–38 8in. and 70–74 5in. shells. The battleship limped out of the battle at slow speed. In addition, gunfire sank destroyer *Akatsuki* and *Yudachi* was sunk by a torpedo hit and gunfire. Four more destroyers received varying degrees of damage.

Amatsukaze was a member of the 19-ship Kagero class. Most of these superb torpedo platforms fought during the Guadalcanal and Solomons campaigns. *Amatsukaze* was in the middle of the action in the first naval battle of Guadalcanal, during which it torpedoed and sank an American destroyer. In return, *Amatsukaze* was heavily damaged by American cruiser gunfire and missed the remainder of the Guadalcanal campaign. (Yamato Museum)

THE FIRST NAVAL BATTLE OF GUADALCANAL, NOVEMBER 13 1942		
	Forces involved	Results
American	2 heavy cruisers, 3 light cruisers, 8 destroyers	2 heavy cruisers heavily damaged, 2 light cruisers sunk, 1 damaged; 4 destroyers sunk, 2 heavily damaged
Japanese	Battleships *Hiei* and *Kirishima*, 1 light cruiser, 11 destroyers	*Hiei* damaged, 2 destroyers sunk, 2 heavily damaged, 2 damaged

Hiei, pictured here in July 1942, was demilitarized in 1929, as required by the Washington Naval Treaty, then rebuilt before the war. This made it the most modern Kongo-class ship, but it still possessed weak protection for a capital ship. In *Hiei*'s first surface action of the Guadalcanal campaign, it was assigned to bombard Henderson Field. During the first naval battle of Guadalcanal, it was the main target of American cruisers and destroyers. Unable to leave the battle area due to damage, it was sunk the following day by American aircraft. *Hiei* was the first Combined Fleet battleship lost in the war. (Naval History and Heritage Command)

When the Japanese commander ordered his force to prematurely withdraw, the battle became a defeat for the Japanese. The cost of this setback increased the next day when *Hiei* was caught near Savo Island while unable to maneuver and sunk by air attack.

As costly as the battle on November 13 was to both sides, it had no decisive result. The Japanese still had to neutralize the airfield to prepare for the arrival of their large convoy. A tentative bombardment by two heavy cruisers on the night of November 13–14 was unsuccessful, so the Combined Fleet ordered another battleship bombardment operation. *Kirishima*, two heavy cruisers, and two destroyer squadrons were assembled and dispatched to crush the airfield in the early hours of November 15. In response, the American commander sent a scratch force to stop the bombardment. This included two modern battleships with the most capable radar-guided fire-control systems in the world. The first battleship action of the war was impending at a decisive moment of the campaign.

THE SECOND NAVAL BATTLE OF GUADALCANAL, NOVEMBER 15 1942		
	Forces involved	Results
American	Battleships *South Dakota* and *Washington*, 4 destroyers	*South Dakota* damaged, 3 destroyers sunk, one heavily damaged
Japanese	Battleship *Kirishima*, 2 heavy cruisers, 1 light cruiser, 9 destroyers	*Kirishima* sunk, 1 heavy cruiser damaged, 1 destroyer sunk

The Japanese commander expected to encounter heavy cruisers, not battleships. His plan was to use his two destroyer squadrons to destroy the American task force, after which his heavy ships would bombard the airfield. The advance destroyers did decimate the American destroyer screen, but soon came under 16in. American battleship fire. In the opening phase of the battle, all four USN destroyers were sunk or crippled, in exchange for a single Japanese destroyer sunk by gunfire.

Content that the path was clear, the Japanese admiral ordered the bombardment to begin. It was then that *South Dakota* loomed out of the darkness. It came

Shown here in a prewar photograph, *Kirishima* was one of the Combined Fleet's most active battleships during the initial period of the war. After participating in both carrier battles during the Guadalcanal campaign, it was committed in November to bombard Henderson Field with its 14in. guns. Running into a modern USN battleship, its light level of protection proved fatal against 16in. naval guns. (Naval History and Heritage Command)

under fire from *Kirishima*, both Japanese heavy cruisers, and two destroyers. Pummelled by 27 topside hits, including a 14in. shell from *Kirishima*, *South Dakota* was knocked out of action. The Japanese also launched 12 Type 93 torpedoes at the battleship, but none hit. While the Japanese focused on *South Dakota*, the *Washington* was tracking *Kirishima* on its radar. From a range of only 8,400yds, *Washington* opened fire, scoring multiple 16in. hits on *Kirishima*. In the final phase of the battle, *Washington* emerged miraculously untouched from a barrage of Type 93s, some fired at short range. *Kirishima* sank later that morning. Henderson Field was untouched, so American aircraft, aided by the carrier *Enterprise*, were able to annihilate the Japanese convoy.

The final naval battle of the Guadalcanal campaign was anticlimactic. Though occurring after Japanese defeat was certain, it displayed the IJN's continuing prowess in night battles.

THE BATTLE OF TASSAFARONGA, NOVEMBER 30 1942		
	Forces involved	Results
American	4 heavy cruisers, 1 light cruiser, 6 destroyers	1 heavy cruiser sunk, 3 heavily damaged
Japanese	8 destroyers	1 destroyer sunk, 1 damaged

Unable to run convoys to Guadalcanal, the only method left to the Japanese to supply their garrison on the island was by destroyer. In the aftermath of their defeat earlier in November, the Combined Fleet planned five Tokyo Express operations to supply the garrison. The first began on the night of November 29 with eight destroyers. The Americans were expecting a Tokyo Express run and had the further benefit of gaining radar detection of the lead Japanese destroyer. Once again, however, the American commander failed to capitalize on his radar advantage. When he opened fire, it was concentrated on the lead Japanese destroyer. It was sunk by a torrent of shells, but not before it had launched its eight Type 93s. One heavy cruiser was struck by two torpedoes, and the next one in line by another. Another 26 Type 93s were launched from other destroyers and hit two more cruisers. *Northampton* was struck by two and later sank.

While the naval campaign raged, the Combined Fleet was conducting another parallel campaign. The Eleventh Air Fleet, principally flying from bases around

Rabaul, was tasked to neutralize Henderson Field. After a tentative start in late August after the Americans brought the airfield into operation, the Eleventh Air Fleet made an all-out effort between September 27 and October 26. The effort ended in failure at the cost of 131 aircraft lost. In total, from August 1 to November 15, 241 aircraft were lost, with a corresponding high loss of aircrew. Compared to the American air units based on Guadalcanal, the Eleventh Air Fleet had numerical superiority. However, given the distance between Rabaul and Henderson Field (565nm), Japanese aircraft were restricted to a single sortie per day. With insufficient numbers of aircraft carrying light bombloads, poor bombing accuracy, and unimaginative tactics, the Japanese never gained real momentum to knock out Henderson Field from the air.

The Solomons Campaign

After the Japanese evacuated Guadalcanal in February 1943, the Americans were still far short of their goal of neutralizing or seizing Rabaul. While the campaign raged on and around Guadalcanal, the Japanese were also fighting a campaign on New Guinea. After their defeat at Guadalcanal, the Japanese decided on a defensive stance when the Americans began to advance in the Central Solomons.

Yamamoto's final operation as commander of the Combined Fleet was a large-scale air campaign to cripple Allied air power, hopefully delaying the start of the

The focal point of the Guadalcanal campaign was Henderson Field, shown here at the start of the campaign. Despite their best efforts, the Japanese were never able to capture the airfield or neutralize it for any lasting period. (Naval History and Heritage Command)

Operation *I* (overleaf)

The third strike of Yamamoto's grand air offensive was directed at Port Moresby on April 12, 1943. It was the largest of the four strikes of Operation *I* and the only one targeted against airfields. The operation required a high degree of coordination, with 54 G4M medium bombers coming from two airfields and 131 Zero fighters coming from four different airfields. The fighter force was divided into two groups. The first was the Air Superiority Force, consisting of 55 Zeros from three carriers flying from bases around Rabaul. The larger Covering Force was allocated 76 Zeros from one additional carrier and three land-based units. The huge formation made a feint toward Milne Bay and then turned right toward Port Moresby. American radar picked up the bombers 83 miles away, giving time to scramble every available Allied fighter. The track of the bombers took them over the Owen Stanley Range of mountains and then to a point northwest of Port Moresby. The Japanese bombed three airfields before hitting Port Moresby, and then struck a fourth airfield before flying back over the Owen Stanleys and back to Rabaul. Allied fighters fought through the Zero escort force to shoot down six G4Ms, and another was so badly damaged it was forced to crash land at Lae. In exchange for the seven G4Ms destroyed, the Allies lost three fighters in air combat and six bombers of various types on the ground. This view shows a *chutai* of G4Ms from the No.705 *Kokutai* which broke off from the main formation to attack the 3-mile Kila Airfield. The bombers have concluded their attack and are headed northeast. Damage to the airfield was light, but the airfield's fuel dump was hit, as is indicated by the large smoke column in this scene.

CENTRAL SOLOMONS CAMPAIGN

American offensive. To accomplish this ambitious objective, Yamamoto ordered the four carriers at Truk to send their air groups to Rabaul. Once joined with the Eleventh Air Fleet already at Rabaul, Yamamoto had over 350 aircraft at his disposal.

Dubbed Operation *I* by the Japanese, the opening move was a fighter sweep over the Russell Islands located to the northwest of Guadalcanal. This failed to weaken American air power at Guadalcanal. The first massed air attack was conducted against shipping off Guadalcanal on April 7. A strike force of 67 dive-bombers was escorted by 157 Zeros. In response, the Americans put up 76 fighters, of which 56 made contact with the Japanese. As dogfights raged between the escorting Zeros and the intercepting American fighters, the dive-bombers did their work, sinking three ships, including a USN destroyer. Twenty-one Japanese aircraft were lost for only seven American losses. After this lone strike, Yamamoto concluded that Allied forces off Guadalcanal had been struck a serious blow.

Next up was a strike against Allied shipping in Oro Bay, New Guinea. A force of 94 Japanese aircraft – 72 Zeros and 22 dive-bombers – attacked on April 11. Three ships were hit, of which a single merchantman was sunk. Six Zeros were lost and no Allied fighters were destroyed. Port Moresby was struck the next day by 131 Zeros escorting 43 G4M bombers. Although the Allies were able to get 44 fighters airborne to intercept, none were able to reach the bombers in the face of the huge Zero escort force. Nevertheless, the Japanese failed to hit a single ship in the harbor and little damage was done to the nearby airfield.

Operation *I* concluded on April 14 with an attack by 188 aircraft on Milne Bay. Only 24 Australian fighters were launched to intercept. Despite excellent bombing conditions, the G4M bombers sunk just a single merchantman and damaged two others.

After only four attacks, Yamamoto called off the operation. Since Japanese aviators claimed excellent results, he was content that the Allied capability to begin offensive operations had been curtailed. In fact, the Allies lost only 25 aircraft and five ships. In return, the Japanese lost 61 aircraft. Operation *I* marked the high-water mark of Japanese air power in the Solomons. Its failure led indirectly to Yamamoto's death, when on April 18 long-range fighters from Guadalcanal shot down the G4M bomber in which he was a passenger over Bougainville in the Northern Solomons.

The first American attack into the Central Solomons began on June 30, 1943, with a landing on Rendova Island. This was planned to be a jumping-off point to invade nearby New Georgia Island, which was the location of the critical airfield at Munda. Against sporadic air attack, the Americans gained a lodgment. The first IJN response did not occur until July 2, when a light cruiser and nine destroyers attempted to bombard the beachhead but hit only adjacent jungle.

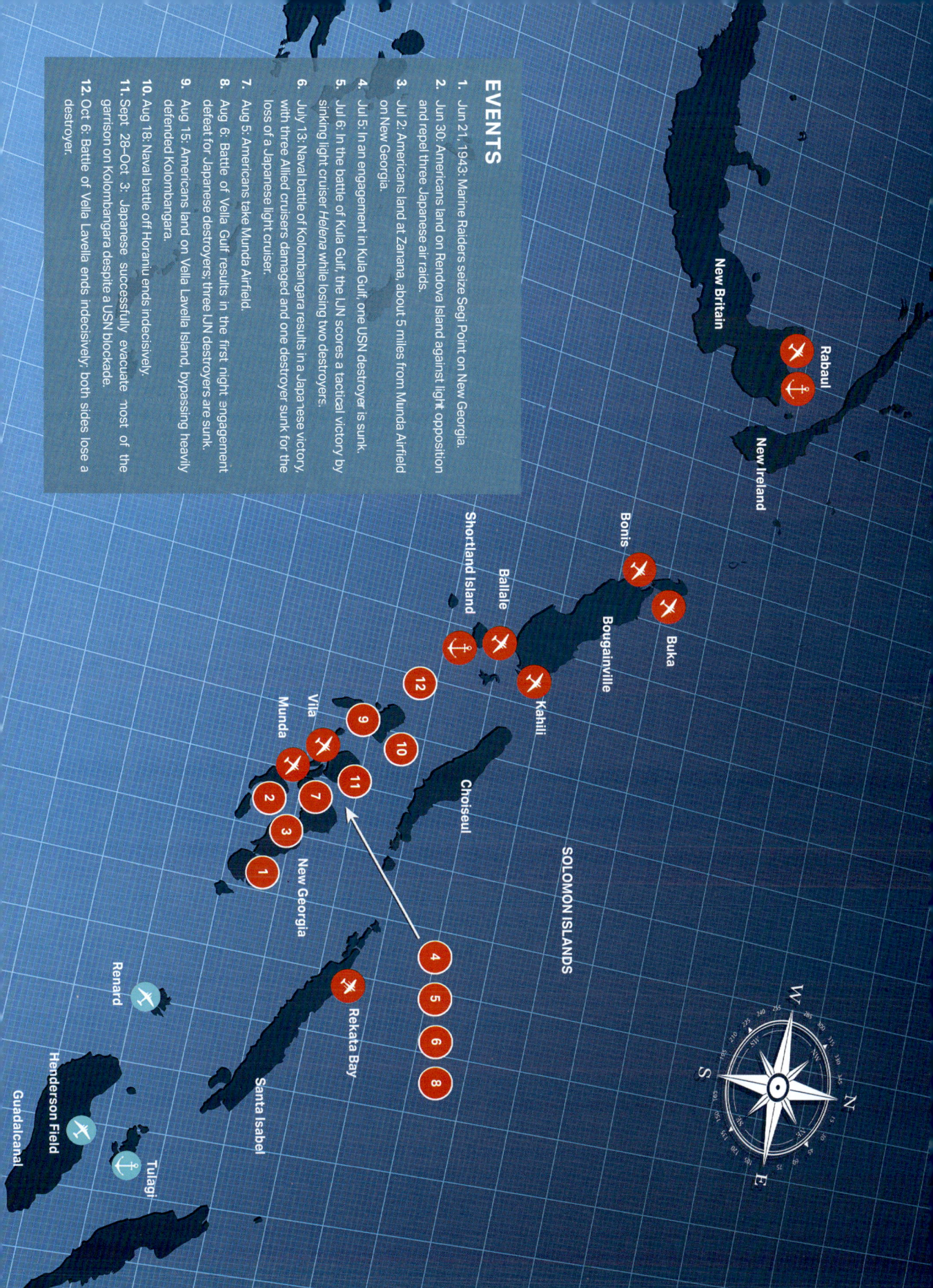

As was often the case in night battles, American radar-directed gunnery focused on a single target. At the battle of Kula Gulf, this target was the large destroyer *Niizuki*, shown here on fire. The Akizuki-class destroyer had only been commissioned in March 1943. (Naval History and Heritage Command)

When the IJA released more troops to defend New Georgia, the only way to move them where they were needed was by destroyer to Kolombangara Island, then by barge to New Georgia. The first run by four destroyers on July 5 met a USN force in Kula Gulf (between Kolombangara and New Georgia). The Japanese commander, recognizing he was vastly outnumbered, ordered a retreat. Before leaving, he sent 14 Type 93s into the gulf. At an incredible 22,000yds, one torpedo hit an American destroyer, which subsequently sank. This was the first of many destroyer actions in the Solomons.

The Americans, receiving intelligence that the Japanese would attempt another reinforcement run the next night, sent a cruiser and destroyer force to stop it. The IJN did intend another such operation with a large force of ten destroyers, led by the new radar-equipped Akizuki-class destroyer *Niizuki*. When the Americans arrived, the Japanese were already inside Kula Gulf. The Japanese were able to discern the presence of the Americans by picking up their radar emissions. When American radar detected the Japanese, the USN commander delayed firing for 16 minutes. The Americans finally opened fire at the lead ship, *Niizuki*, and struck it repeatedly; it later sank. As often happened in night battles, USN radar-guided gunfire focused on a single target. The next two Japanese destroyers fired a full salvo of 16 Type 93s at the easily visible American cruisers. Three struck *Helena*, which broke in two. *Helena* was the largest ship lost in the Solomons campaign. After the initial phase of the clash, American gunnery damaged several other destroyers. One ran aground and was sunk by American aircraft the following day. Having succeeded in delivering troops and supplies and sinking a light cruiser in the process, the action was a tactical victory for the Japanese.

THE BATTLE OF KULA GULF, JULY 6 1943		
	Forces involved	Results
American	3 light cruisers, 4 destroyers	1 light cruiser sunk
Japanese	10 destroyers	2 destroyers sunk, 5 damaged

On July 9, the Japanese made an uncontested run with three cruisers and four destroyers to move troops to Kolombangara. The next run, which began on July 12, prompted the second major naval battle of the campaign. A reinforced

American task force was present, but used the same plan which made no allowance for the capabilities of the Type 93 torpedo.

THE BATTLE OF KOLOMBANGARA, JULY 13 1943

	Forces involved	Results
Allied	3 light cruisers (1 New Zealand), 10 destroyers	3 light cruisers heavily damaged, 1 destroyer sunk, 2 damaged
Japanese	1 light cruiser, 5 destroyers	Light cruiser *Jintsu* sunk

The battle of Kolombangara was a virtual repeat of the action at Kula Gulf. The Americans had ample warning of the approach of the Japanese, but again failed to take advantage. The Japanese used passive detectors to track the advance of the Americans and get off a salvo of 29 Type 93s in the early hours of July 13. Before the arrival of the Japanese torpedoes, the Allied light cruisers were able to unleash a torrent of 6in. shells at Japanese flagship *Jintsu*. Hit by innumerable shells, it sank with the loss of 482 crewmen. No other Japanese ship was hit. One of the Type 93s in the first barrage hit and crippled the New Zealand cruiser *Leander*. After reloading, the Japanese fired another barrage of 31 Type 93s. This was even more devastating – each American light cruiser was hit by a torpedo and knocked out of the war until November, and a destroyer was sunk. The quick reaction of the well-drilled Japanese destroyer crews secured another victory for the Combined Fleet.

On July 2, the Americans made their landing on New Georgia, but efforts to secure the airfield at Munda quickly ran into trouble. Japanese resistance in

Long Lance in Action (overleaf)

On July 6, 1943, the Combined Fleet mounted a major resupply operation for the Japanese garrison on New Georgia in the Central Solomons. It was intercepted by an American force of three light cruisers and four destroyers. The Japanese force, under the command of Rear Admiral Akiyama Teruo (commander of the 3rd Destroyer Squadron), included a support group of Akiyama's flagship, the new destroyer *Niizuki*, the Kagero-class destroyer *Tanikaze*, and the Shiratsuyu-class destroyer *Suzukaze*, which was providing cover for seven destroyers in two transport groups. The Japanese arrived in Kula Gulf first and had begun unloading their cargos when radar on *Niizuki* detected what Akiyama thought was a group of American ships. Though the Japanese radar contact was probably not valid, radar on the USN cruiser *Honolulu* did gain contact on the Japanese at 0136hrs at over 20,000yds. Confusion and indecision by the American commander prevented the Americans from opening fire until 0157hrs from about 7,000yds. All three American cruisers targeted the lead Japanese ship, *Niizuki*, which was hit and crippled within a few minutes. Behind Akiyama's flagship were *Suzukaze* and *Tanikaze*, which within seconds of the Americans opening fire, both launched a full salvo of torpedoes at the American cruisers. This scene depicts the moment when the two Japanese destroyers launched their eight Type 93 torpedoes, while *Niizuki* is deluged in fire and has already started to burn. The action ended in a Japanese triumph when three Type 93s hit the cruiser *Helena* and broke it in half. *Niizuki* also sank and Akiyama was killed, and several other destroyers were damaged by gunfire. Later that day, a second Japanese destroyer was lost when it ran aground off Kolombangara Island and was later destroyed by aircraft.

NORTHERN SOLOMONS CAMPAIGN

excellent defensive terrain stopped the attack cold. After regrouping and pushing additional troops into the battle, the attack was resumed on July 25. This time, the weight of American firepower made itself felt and the Japanese decided to withdraw from New Georgia. Following their withdrawal, the Japanese expected Kolombangara to be the next American target. Not wanting a repeat of the slugfest on New Georgia, the Americans decided to bypass Kolombangara and land on Vella Lavella Island some 35nm to the northwest. The landing there on August 15 was unopposed; this surprise operation completely unhinging the Japanese defense of the Central Solomons.

During the run-up to the American landing on Vella Lavella, the Japanese were intent on reinforcing Kolombangara. On July 19, the Combined Fleet changed its tactics and committed three heavy cruisers to another reinforcement operation. The heavy ships were meant to inflict a sharp defeat on any USN attempt to interdict the operation. Instead, the operation was a minor disaster, with two destroyers sunk by air attack and one of the heavy cruisers and a destroyer damaged. Two reinforcement operations to the western side of Kolombangara were successful, on July 22 and August 1. A repeat operation was planned for August 6, resulting in the next major naval clash.

THE BATTLE OF VELLA GULF, AUGUST 6–7 1943		
	Forces involved	Results
Allied	6 destroyers	No damage
Japanese	4 destroyers	3 destroyers sunk

Whereas the Japanese applied the same tactics and used the same routes, several sharp defeats had forced the USN to rethink matters. The Americans decided it was foolish to chase destroyers with cruisers at night in confined waters, so now led their operations with destroyers under more aggressive commanders. A major change in tactics was to build their battle plan on radar-guided night torpedo attacks. As predicted by the senior officer on the only Japanese destroyer to survive the battle, repeating the same operation again was courting disaster. American radar picked up the approaching Japanese at 19,700yds. When the range closed to 6,300yds, 22 torpedoes left the tubes on three destroyers and headed for the oblivious Japanese. Three of the four Japanese ships were hit by torpedoes, the fourth only surviving because a torpedo went through its rudder without exploding. For the first time in the war, Japanese destroyers lost a night action.

On the night of August 17–18, there was an indecisive destroyer action between two equal forces of four destroyers when the Japanese tried to move reinforcements to the northeastern part of Vella Lavella. On September 18, the

THE COMBINED FLEET'S NOVEMBER CONVOY

Americans completed the capture of the island. The Japanese then changed strategy: the Central Solomons were only to be held until late September–early October, allowing time for the defenses on Bougainville in the Northern Solomons to be strengthened. Over 12,000 men were trapped on Kolombangara, whom the Japanese intended to evacuate by barge and destroyer. This was achieved despite persistent American efforts to stop the retreat.

The next clash was prompted by a Japanese operation to evacuate their remaining troops from Vella Lavella. Six American destroyers were ordered to intercept the Japanese evacuation force, but only three made contact. These were able to get 14 torpedoes in the water, followed by a gunnery attack. The nearest Japanese destroyer was struck by five shells, but not before it had a chance to launch a salvo of eight torpedoes. One hit an American destroyer, which later sank. The American force disintegrated when a second destroyer was hit by another Type 93 barrage, and a third destroyer collided with the first destroyer hit by torpedoes. Since the Japanese were able to withdraw their men from Vella Lavella and had inflicted more damage than they received, this was another tactical victory for the IJN. Exchanging one destroyer for another, though, was not an exchange rate the Japanese could sustain.

THE BATTLE OF VELLA LAVELLA, OCTOBER 6 1943		
	Forces involved	Results
American	3 destroyers	1 destroyer sunk, 1 badly damaged, 1 damaged
Japanese	6 destroyers	1 destroyer sunk

The largest naval battle of the Solomons campaign came as a result of the American invasion of Bougainville on November 1. The Japanese were aware that an American landing on Bougainville was imminent but were caught by surprise regarding its location. On November 1, two Japanese air attacks on the invasion force in Empress Augusta Bay in northwestern Bougainville were ineffective. Alarmed over this latest American invasion so near to Rabaul, the Combined Fleet ordered its first major operation in the South Pacific since the conclusion of the Guadalcanal campaign. A force built around heavy cruisers *Myoko* and *Haguro* was sent to attack the invasion force. The Japanese commander did not expect to encounter major American surface forces, just defenseless transports. This nonsensical

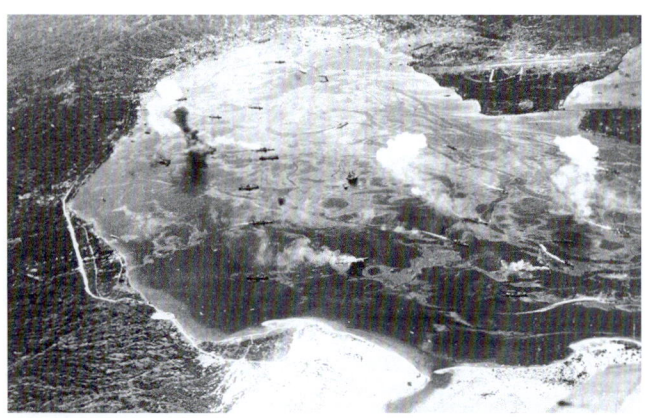

This photograph shows the American carrier air raid against the Second Fleet in Simpson Harbor on November 5, 1943. Koga had ordered seven heavy cruisers, one light cruiser, and four destroyers from Truk to Rabaul for another attack on the American beachhead on Bougainville. Four of the cruisers were damaged, bringing the threat to the beachhead to an end. (Naval History and Heritage Command)

EVENTS

A major part of the Combined Fleet's November offensive was the movement of a major convoy to Guadalcanal. On November 14, 1942, the attempt ended in failure.

1. 0700hrs: An American dive-bomber spots the Japanese convoy 150 miles from Guadalcanal
2. 0900hrs: Two dive-bombers launch the first attack on the convoy but score no hits.
3. 1250–1302hrs: 38 aircraft from Henderson Field attack. Despite the presence of defending Zeros, two transports are torpedoed and later sink. Another is hit by bombs and forced to return to Shortland Island.
4. 1430hrs: Five dive-bombers attack and claim hits on two transports.
5. 1450hrs: Additional dive-bombers claim hits on three different transports; one later sinks.
6. Approximately 1450hrs: Seven B-17 heavy bombers are engaged by Japanese fighters; no hits are made.
7. 1530hrs: *Enterprise* aircraft hit two transports; both are abandoned and later sink.
8. 1530hrs: Eight B-17s bomb from high altitude but score no hits.
9. 1620hrs: Japanese fighters defeat a dive-bombing attack.
10. 1723–1738hrs: 34 aircraft from Henderson Field attack in the face of 14 defending Japanese fighters. One transport is set on fire and abandoned.
11. Nov 15, 0400hrs: last four transports run aground on Guadalcanal.

assumption was proven incorrect when the battle opened with an American destroyer torpedo attack in the early hours of November 2.

Though the initial barrage of 25 American torpedoes met with no success when the Japanese commander ordered a well-timed course change, the opening gunnery attack from the four fast-firing light cruisers pummeled light cruiser *Sendai*. Struck repeatedly, it was left dead in the water. The two destroyers in the column behind the cruiser collided.

THE BATTLE OF EMPRESS AUGUSTA BAY, NOVEMBER 2 1943		
	Forces involved	Results
American	4 light cruisers, 8 destroyers	2 light cruisers damaged, 1 destroyer heavily damaged, 4 damaged
Japanese	2 heavy cruisers, 2 light cruisers, 6 destroyers	1 light cruiser and 1 destroyer sunk, 2 heavy cruisers damaged, 2 destroyers damaged

In the gunnery phase, two of the American light cruisers were hit by 8in. shells. Luckily for the Americans, all failed to explode. The adept maneuvering of the American commander neutralized the Type 93 threat. In the final phase of the action, the wounded *Sendai* was finished off and another Japanese destroyer damaged by collision was sunk by American destroyers.

The battle of Empress Augusta Bay was an impressive American victory. The scratch Japanese force was unable to maneuver effectively, failed to use its destroyers aggressively, and shot poorly. After the failure of this operation, Combined Fleet headquarters was so concerned about the American lodgment on Bougainville that Admiral Koga ordered the dispatch of the Second Fleet, with seven heavy cruisers and a destroyer squadron, to Rabaul to crush the beachhead. An American carrier strike caught the force refueling in Simpson Harbor on the morning of November 5, damaging four heavy and two light cruisers and a destroyer. The Second Fleet left the same day to return to Truk, marking the IJN's last major foray into the South Pacific.

The last naval engagement of the campaign took place on November 25, when a Japanese destroyer force was intercepted carrying reinforcements to northern Bougainville. In the resulting battle of Cape St George, the deterioration of Japanese night-fighting skills was on full display. An American destroyer force of equal strength gained radar contact on the approaching Japanese at long range. Not until the range had closed to 5,500yds did the American commander give the order to unleash his torpedoes. Two destroyers were hit in this initial attack, then the Americans chased down the three survivors, sinking one of them.

THE BATTLE OF CAPE ST GEORGE, NOVEMBER 25 1943		
	Forces involved	Results
American	5 destroyers	No damage
Japanese	5 destroyers	3 destroyers sunk, 1 damaged

ANALYSIS

On August 1, 1942, just before the start of the Guadalcanal campaign, the Combined Fleet held a slight numerical edge over the USN in the Pacific. At the conclusion of the Solomons campaign at the end of November 1943, the Combined Fleet was in a definite position of inferiority compared to the USN. During this time, the Combined Fleet had suffered heavy losses – one carrier, three battleships, three heavy and four light cruisers, 44 destroyers, and 33 submarines. In addition, it had lost the bulk of its highly trained aircrews. Furthermore, the Japanese failed to stop the American advance through the Solomons. Rabaul had been neutralized as a major base and the next phase of the war, during which Japan's inner defenses were under threat, was about to begin.

To a large degree, the IJN's increasingly desperate straits were unavoidable. Japan was simply unable to replace the Combined Fleet's losses, while American industrial capacity allowed the USN to not only cover its losses but to grow stronger each month.

Still, the Combined Fleet did make the most of its window of opportunity to stop the first USN offensive of the war before the disparity in industrial capacities between Japan and the United States made itself fully apparent. In August 1942, the Combined Fleet still enjoyed a quantitative and qualitative edge over the USN. The problem was Yamamoto's failure to identify the struggle for Guadalcanal as a critical battle that Japan had to win to prove the viability of its defensive strategy. Failure to identify the importance of the battle translated into piecemeal commitment of forces to it. At no point during the six-month campaign did Yamamoto make an all-out commitment of the Combined Fleet's remaining strength. The Americans did commit all available forces, and this was always just enough to defeat the latest Japanese attempt to retake the island.

The airfield on Guadalcanal became the fulcrum for the entire campaign, with American ground, naval, and air forces focused on holding the airfield and keeping it operational. Despite their numerical advantages, the Japanese were never able to mass their forces to seize the airfield or knock it out of action for a prolonged period. Possession of Henderson Field ultimately proved decisive in securing victory in the campaign for the United States.

Combined Fleet operations were not well designed during the campaign. The first example was the Japanese offensive in August. Mounting a major fleet operation to move a convoy of 1,500 troops to the island highlighted that the Japanese did not understand the dimensions of the campaign battle in which they were engaged. While the Combined Fleet's increased commitment in October gained it an important advantage by temporarily neutralizing the airfield and getting most of a convoy to the island, it was insufficient to gain victory. Even victory in the carrier battle of Santa Cruz was not enough to prevent the USN from maintaining its robust support of the American garrison on Guadalcanal. It was probably at this point that the Combined Fleet had its biggest advantage, but Yamamoto failed to seize the moment.

Only two Combined Fleet carriers were available in November 1942 after the battle of Santa Cruz, making the battle a shallow victory for the Japanese. This is one of those ships, *Junyo*, shown here after the war. Fighters from *Junyo* were unable to protect the pivotal November convoy. (Naval History and Heritage Command)

The next major effort in November was poorly synchronized and the result was catastrophic. Yamamoto once more resorted to a battleship bombardment of the airfield, but again it was assigned to the least powerful battleships in the Combined Fleet. When the first bombardment failed on the night of November 12–13, another attempt was ordered with only a single battleship. Incredibly, Yamamoto let the convoy advance toward Guadalcanal after the initial bombardment operation failed and before the second one could even be attempted. Aircraft from Henderson Field and from the carrier *Enterprise* were able to attack the convoy, sinking six transports and forcing another back. After the second bombardment force was turned back on the night of November 14–15, the Americans were able to finish the destruction of the convoy.

Yamamoto's reluctance to commit his battleships in the waters off Guadalcanal was a key decision. Given the pivotal importance of Henderson Field and the demonstrated ability of Japanese battleships to badly damage it, an aggressive commitment of battleships could have turned the campaign. There were two major reasons for Yamamoto's failure to do so. One was the orthodoxy of the Combined Fleet's staff in terms of its thinking on the proper employment of battleships. To them, these were capital units and were only committed if a decisive action was likely. Such ships could not be risked in the closed waters off Guadalcanal, especially at night. The other possible reason was a concern for the fuel requirements of such an operation.

Of course, the Japanese did employ battleships to bombard Henderson Field on three occasions. On all three occasions, Kongo-class units were employed. As the oldest battleships in the fleet, they were viewed as more expendable. Furthermore, their extensive prewar training in night combat made them more suited and more survivable. The loss of *Hiei* to air power from Henderson Field would seem to support Yamamoto's reluctance to expose slower battleships to air attack. Given the relatively small scale of American air power at Henderson, which had difficulty sinking the previously damaged *Hiei*, the employment of the better-protected Nagato class or even a Yamato-class super-battleship would have likely been effective in neutralizing the airfield and withstanding its counterattack. While the fuel factor was important, the author believes that this was an excuse. Sufficient fuel could have been found to send *Yamato* to Guadalcanal if its employment was expected to be decisive. The real failing was a lack of imagination. Without it, there was no way the Combined Fleet was going to risk its most impressive ships just to bombard an airfield.

So steep were losses at Guadalcanal that the ensuing Solomons campaign was conducted without any thought by Yamamoto or his successor to committing the main strength of the Combined Fleet. Yamamoto's last offensive – Operation *I* – was a total failure. The days of simply massing air power against Allied targets to inflict significant blows in a single attack were gone. It is inconceivable that Yamamoto believed that only four attacks would render operational-level results by crippling Allied offensive power in the region. The operation was poorly planned and marked by poor target selection, dispersal of effort, and lack of follow-up. The Japanese had yet to understand that to be effective, air power must be applied in a concerted manner over time, not just in a few "decisive" raids. Operation *I* provided another example of Yamamoto's inability to mass forces on the objective of operational importance.

The Solomons campaign was a Japanese success at the strategic level since it took the Americans from February to November 1943 to advance the roughly 400nm from Guadalcanal to Bougainville. In this context, Japanese economy of force operations in the Central and Northern Solomons looked like a wise investment. At the operational level, the cost of the campaign was still high for the Japanese. The Combined Fleet's destroyers took the lead in the Solomons campaign and suffered correspondingly heavy losses. For the remainder of the war, the Combined Fleet struggled with a shortage of fleet destroyers. This was apparent during the major fleet actions in the Philippine Sea in June 1944 and in the Philippines in October 1944, when inadequate destroyer screens contributed to the heavy losses inflicted by American submarines on the Combined Fleet.

Another area of weakness was the Combined Fleet's carrier-based air power. At the beginning of the Guadalcanal campaign, the carrier force was rebuilt following the Midway debacle. At this point, the overall quality of Japanese carrier aircrews was still high. Victory at Santa Cruz was proof that their carrier aircrews still possessed the determination and skills to inflict serious losses on the USN's carrier force. However, in the face of continual losses, this changed dramatically by the end of the Solomons campaign. Even as the Combined Fleet decided to withhold the carrier air groups during the campaign, both Yamamoto and Koga relented at certain points and committed them, hoping for decisive results. This failed to materialize, and more irreplaceable carrier aircrew veterans were lost. The downward trajectory of the quality of Japanese carrier aircrews was epitomized by the 173 aircraft sent to Rabaul on November 1, 1943. On November 2, 100 of these aircraft attacked the USN force which had just won the battle of Empress Augusta Bay. Despite the American force of four light cruisers and eight destroyers having no air cover for most of the action, the Japanese were only able to place two bomb hits on the stern of a light cruiser, causing little damage. On November 11, the supposedly elite Japanese carrier aircrews mounted a major assault on an American carrier force of two fleet carriers and a light carrier attacking Rabaul. The Japanese attack force consisted of 27 dive-bombers and 14 torpedo planes, with an escort of 67 Zeros. Twenty of the dive-bombers managed to attack the carriers; all three carriers endured near misses by bombs, but none were hit. Only three dive-bombers survived the combined efforts of the defending American fighters and antiaircraft fire. The 14 torpedo planes followed next – all were shot down, with no success. By November 13 (having arrived at Rabaul on the 1st), the elite carrier air groups had suffered the loss of 50 percent of their fighters, 85 percent of their dive-bombers, and 50 percent of their torpedo planes. Such losses had a dramatic effect. When, later in November, the USN launched an amphibious assault of the Gilbert Islands, the Combined Fleet's carrier force was in no condition to respond. Indeed, the carrier air groups would never recover. After being rebuilt by June 1944 in time for the decisive battle in the defense of the Marianas, the result was the near total destruction of the Japanese carrier air groups in the largest carrier battle of the war.

In terms of the fundamentals of naval warfare, the Combined Fleet was unable to compete with the growing prowess of the USN. In the opening months of the Pacific War, and even into the first phase of the Guadalcanal campaign, the Combined Fleet possessed an excellent naval air arm with significant striking power against surface ships. By November 1943, Japanese naval air forces proved impotent against maritime targets. Japanese surface warfare capabilities were buoyed by impressive night-fighting tactics. In the initial phases of the Guadalcanal campaign, the Combined Fleet could count on its night-fighting skills to carry the day. This remained the case up until the end of the Guadalcanal campaign, despite occasions where American tenacity or radar began to corrode the Combined Fleet's edge in night fighting. In the initial night battles in the Solomons campaign, the Americans failed to

An RO-100-class submarine photographed near Rabaul on March 16, 1943, by an Allied aircraft. These 600-ton submarines were well suited for operations in the Solomons. However, only a few of the 18 boats in the class even reported an attempted attack against an enemy target, and all but one was lost. (Naval History and Heritage Command)

appreciate the full capabilities of the formidable Type 93 torpedo, paying dearly for this lack of insight. By the end of the campaign, the full incorporation of radar into American tactics and a new generation of aggressive leaders totally turned the tables on the Japanese at night. Though night battles were rare for the remainder of the war, when they occurred, the USN usually demonstrated its superiority.

As the Combined Fleet lost its edge in naval air power and night fighting, it also fell behind in other key areas. Japanese deficiencies in fleet air defense became more apparent and more costly as the weight of American air power increased throughout 1943. Japanese antisubmarine capabilities failed to keep pace with American technological advances on their submarines, which were operated with better tactics and by more aggressive submarine captains. In 1943, shipping losses were double that of new additions, reducing the size of Japan's merchant fleet by almost one million tons. In 1944, merchant losses reached catastrophic proportions. Combined with the decline in warfare skills was a continuing negligence of intelligence and weakness in logistics. Whereas the Combined Fleet could still be considered superior to the USN in many areas in mid-1942, by the end of 1943 it could no longer compete with the USN in any warfare area. If 1943 was a year of rough parity, it led to a string of disasters in 1944 which marked the end of the Combined Fleet as an effective force.

FURTHER READING

Evans, David C. & Peattie, Mark R., *Kaigun*, Naval Institute Press, Annapolis (1997)
Frank, Richard B., *Guadalcanal*, Random House, New York (1990)
Jentchura, Hansgeorg, Jung, Dieter & Mickel, Peter, *Warships of the Imperial Japanese Navy 1869–1945*, Naval Institute Press, Annapolis (1977)
Lundstrom, John B., *Black Shoe Carrier Admiral*, Naval Institute Press, Annapolis (2006)
Lundstrom, John B., *The First Team and the Guadalcanal Campaign*, Naval Institute Press, Annapolis (1994)
O'Hara, Vincent P., Dickson, W. David & Worth, Richard, *On Seas Contested*, Naval Institute Press, Annapolis (2010)
Peattie, Mark R., *Nan'yo*, University of Hawaii Press, Honolulu (1988)
Peattie, Mark R., *Sunburst*, Naval Institute Press, Annapolis (2001)
United States Strategic Bombing Survey, *The Reduction of Truk*, Naval Analysis Division (1947)
Watts, Anthony J., *Japanese Warships of World War II*, Doubleday & Company, Garden City (1970)
www.combinedfleet.com

INDEX

Note: Page locators in bold refer to captions, plates and pictures.

air superiority 9, 30, **40**
aircraft 18, **23**, 40, **59**, 76
    Aichi D3A1 Type 99 (IJN) 29, **30**, 64, 78
    Mitsubishi A6M2 Type 0 (Zero) (IJN) 29–30, **30**, **40**, **53**, **(61)62–63**, 64, 78
    Mitsubishi G3M2 Type 96 (IJN) 30, **30**
    Mitsubishi G4M1 Type 1 (IJN) 30, **30**, **50**, **53**, **(61)62–63**, 64
    Nakajima B5N2 Type 97 (IJN) 28, 29, **29**, 30, 78
    Yokosuka E14Y (IJN) 40
airfields 6, 14, 43, 46, **49**, 50, **50**, 51, **(61)62–63**, 64, 67
    Henderson Field, Guadalcanal 8–9, **8**, 10, 12, **26**, **27**, 43, 54, **(55)56–57**, 58, **59**, 60, **60**, 61, 75, 76–77
Akiyama, Rear Adm Teruo **67**
Australian Army, the 5, 12, 50, 51

Battle of Cape Esperance, the 9, 42, **42**, 54, **54**
Battle of Cape St George, the 74, **74**
Battle of Empress Augusta Bay, the **13**, 14, **14**, **20**, 21, **36**, 72–**74**, **74**, 78
Battle of Guadalcanal (First), the **26**, 58–59, **58**, **59**
Battle of Guadalcanal (Second), the **20**, 59, **59**
Battle of Kolombangara, the **23**, **35**, 66–67, **67**, 70
Battle of Kula Gulf, the **5**, **23**, 43, **48**, 66, **66**
Battle of Midway, the 4, 6, 17, 18, 29, 37, 77
Battle of Santa Cruz, the 10, 37, **38–39**, 42, 54–55, **55**, 75, **76**, 77
Battle of Savo Island, the **8**, **8**, **19**, 22, 42, 52, **52**, **53**, 54
Battle of Tassafaronga, the 12, **60**, 60–61
Battle of the Bismarck Sea, the 44
Battle of the Coral Sea, the 4, 6, 12, 16, 29
Battle of the Eastern Solomons, the 8, 37, **53**, 53–54
Battle of the Java Sea, the 26, 28
Battle of Vella Gulf, the **70**
Battle of Vella Lavella, the 72, **72**
Bougainville 4, 9, 13, 14, 31, 43, 44, 50, 72–74

carrier aircrews 77–78
catapults 17, 18
communications security and code-breaking 43–44
conversions and upgrades 16, 17, 18, 19, 20, **32**, 47
    hybrid carrier-battleship conversions 17–18

escort protection 9, 14, 17, 22, **23**, 29, 30, **30**, 33, 44, 47, 53, **53**, **55**, **61**, 64, 78

fire control systems 25–26, 27, 36, 59
fuel supplies 46, 49–50, 51, 77

Guadalcanal campaign, the 6–12, **10**, **32**, 34, **35**, 36, **36**, 37, **40**, 41–43, **42**, **53**, 58, **58**, **61**, 75, 78

HF/DF (high-frequency direction finding) 41, 48–49

IJA (Imperial Japanese Army), the 5, 8, 9, 10, 12, 13, 14, 30, 42, 43, 51, 54, 66
IJN (Imperial Japanese Navy), the 4, 5, 8, 9, 10, 12, 13–14, **16**, 17–18, 26, 27, 28, 30, 40, 41, 43, 44, 47, 48, 49–50, 66
    1st Combined Communications Unit 41
    Battleship Divisions 33
    battleships 17–18, **17**, **32**, 76–77
        Fuso 17, **32**
        Haruna **27**, **33**, 54, **(55)56–57**
        Hiei 26, **33**, **58**, **58**, 59, **59**, 76–77
        Hyuga 18, **32**
        Ise 18, **25**, **32**
        Kirishima 26, **33**, 59, **59**, 60, **60**
        Kongo 17, **25**, **27**, **32**, **33**, 54, **(55)56–57**, 76
        Musashi 18, **18**, 34, **47**, 49
        Nagato **18**, **25**, **32**, 50, 77
        Yamato 18, **18**, **25**, **25**, 32, 33, 34, 40, 49, **55**, 77
    Carrier Divisions 33
    carriers 16, **16**, 36
        Chiyoda (carrier) 16–17
        Hosho (carrier) 16

        Junyo 55, **55**, **76**
        Kaiyo (carrier) 17, **47**
        Ryuho (carrier) 16, **33**, **47**
        Ryujo (carrier) 16, **33**, 53, **53**
        Shoho (carrier) 16
        Shokaku (carrier) **16**, 29, **33**, 37, **53**, 55, **55**
        Taiyo (carrier) 17
        Zuiho 16, 17, **33**, **55**
    Combined Fleet Organization **32**–**34**, 36, **45**
        Eighth Fleet 8, **8**, 19, 24, **32**, **33**, **34**, 52
        Eleventh Air Fleet **32**, 60–61, 64
        Fifth Fleet **33**–**34**
        First Fleet **32**–**33**
        Fourth Fleet **33**
        Second Fleet 24, **33**, 34, 36, 44, **72**, 74
        Sixth Fleet **34**
        Third Fleet 24, **32**, **33**, 34, 36
    Cruiser Divisions **32**, 33
        6th **19**, **32**
    Destroyer Squadrons **32**–**33**, **34**, 35, 47, **67**
    destroyers **5**, 21–24, **25**, **32**, 36, 50, 60, 64, 66, 77
        Abukuma **34**
        Akatsuki 58
        Akizuki 24, **25**
        Amatsukaze **58**
        Asashio 23, **23**
        Fubuki 22, 42
        Jintsu **33**, **35**, 67, **67**
        Mikasuki **23**
        Naganami **13**
        Nagara **33**
        Nagatsuki **48**
        Niizuki 66, **66**, **(67)68–69**
        Shimakaze 23
        Suzukaze **(67)68–69**
        Tanikaze **(67)68–69**
        Yugumo 23
        Yura 33
    gunnery **25**, 25–26
    heavy cruisers 9, 14, 18–20, **25**, **25**, **27**, 28, **32**, **33**, 35, 43, 44, **46**, **52**, **53**, 54, **54**, **55**, 59, **59**, 60, 70, **72**, **74**, **74**
        Atago **26**, **26**, 33
        Chikuma 26, 53
        Chokai **8**, 19, 33
        Haguro **14**, 19, **33**, 72
        Kako 19, 33
        Mogami 18, 19–20, 33
        Myoko 19, **25**, **33**, **36**, 72
        Takao 19, 26, **26**
        Tone 20, 26, **33**
    light cruisers 14, 20–21, **20**, **33**, **46**, **55**, **58**, **59**, 64, **67**, **72**, **74**
        Katori **34**
        Oyodo 21, **47**
        Sendai **20**, 21, **34**, 74
    No. 705 *Kokutai* **(61)** **62–63**
    repair ships 49, 51
    Submarine Squadrons **34**
    submarines 24, **24**, 37
        RO-100-class submarine 78
    transports 9, 10, 12, **14**, 17, 22, 24, 44, **48**, 54, 58, **67**, 76
        Yamazaki Maru **10**
intelligence 6–8, 37–43, 66, 79

Japanese strategy 4–9, **8**, **10**, 10–14, 25, 26, 28, 30, 31, **33**, 34, 35–37, 41–43, 44, 52–53, 54, 58, 59, 61–64, 66, 70, 72, **72**, 74, 75–77, 79

Koga, Adm Mineichi 4, 14, 31–34, **33**, 44, **72**, 74, 77
Kurita, Rear Adm Takeo **55**

logistics and supplies 12, 13, 37, 44–51, **49**, 60, **67**, 77, 79
losses 4, 10, 12, 14, 15, 16, **17**, 18, **19**, **20**, 21, 22, **22**, 24, **24**, 29, 30, **32**, **33**, **34**, **35**, 37, 47, 51, 52, 53, **53**, **54**, 55, **55**, 58, **58**, **59**, 60, 61, 64, 66, 67, **67**, 72, **72**, **74**, 75, 77, 78

maps 7, **11**, **65**, **71**, **73**
merchant shipping 47–48, 79
Mikawa, Vice-Adm Gunichi 8, 52–53
military strength and complements 4, 15–16, **15**, 17, **17**, **19**, 20, **22**, 24, **24**, 29, **34**, 42, 47, **52**, **53**, **54**, **55**, **58**, **59**, **60**, **66**, **67**, **70**, **72**, **74**, 75, 78
modifications 18, 20, 21, 23, **48**
muzzle velocities 25, **25**, 27

Nagumo, Vice-Adm Chuichi 53, 54, 55
Nakajima, Cmdr Chikataka 40
naval districts of the Japanese Home Islands 46
naval exercises **19**, 20
naval treaty restrictions 16, 17, 18, 19, 21, 23, 59
New Georgia 67–70, **67**
night actions 9, 10, 14, 19, 22, 26, 28, 35, 36, 42, 52, 54, **54**, 58, 60, **66**, 70, 74, 76, 78–79
Nimitz, Adm Chester 6
November Convoy, the **10**, 59, 76, **76**

Operation *I* (April 12, 1943) 31, 61–64, **(61)62–63**, 77

Papuan Peninsula, New Guinea 12–13
Pearl Harbor attack, the 29, **29**, 31
Port Moresby, New Guinea 6, 12, **(61)62–63**, 64
production 15, 22, 23, 24, 47, **47**
protection 17, 18, 19, 20, 22, 25, 29, 30, **59**, 60

Rabaul 4–5, 13, 14, **34**, **40**, 46, **49**, **50**, 50–51, 61
radar 26, 36, 37, 49, 52, 54, 58, 59, 60, 66, **66**, **67**, 70, 74, 78–79
ranges **25**, **25**, 26, 27, **27**, 28, **28**, 30, **30**, 36, 54, **55**, 60, 66, **67**, 70, 74
reconnaissance 40, 42
repairs and maintenance 46–47, **46**, 48, 49, 50, 51
Royal Navy, the 15, 30, 46

Seletar Naval Base, Singapore 46
Solomons campaign, the, 4, **5**, 12–14, **18**, 21, 22, **30**, **32**, **33**, 34, 35, 36, **36**, 44, **47**, **48**, 61–72, **(61)62–63**, **65**, **66**, **(67)68–69**, **71**, **75**, 77, 78
South Pacific bases **7**
speeds 18, 19, 21, 22, 23, 29, **30**
stability issues 20, 23

Tokyo Express runs 9, 10, 12, 60
training 24–25, **34**, 35, 76
Truk Atoll 18, **18**, **21**, 34, 46, 48–50, **49**
Tulagi, South Solomon Islands 6
Type 88 binoculars (IJN) 35

US strategy 4, 9, 12–13, 44, 60, 61, 64, 66, 67, 70, 75, 78–79
USAAF, the **14**, **23**, 44, **50**, 51
USMC (US Marine Corps), the 9, 42
USN (US Navy), the 4, 6, 8, 9, 12, 15, **15**, 17, 18, 20, 21, 24, 26, 28, **33**, **34**, **35**, 37, 41, 42, 43, 52, 54, **54**, 58, 59, **60**, 75, 77, 78–79
    Enterprise (carrier) 42, 53, **53**, 55, **55**, 60, 76
    Helena (light cruiser) **43**, 66, **67**
    Hornet (carrier) **29**, 54, 55, 55
    South Dakota (battleship) 59–60, **59**
    submarines **19**, 79
    Washington (battleship) **59**, 60

Washington Naval Treaty, the 19, **59**
weaponry 17, 18, 19, 20, 21, 22, 23, 24, **25**, 27, **51**, 54, 55, **55**, **60**
    antiaircraft 22, 25, 26–27, **27**
    Type 89 twin-gun (IJN) 27
    torpedoes
        Type 91 (IJN) 28, **28**, 29
        Type 93 torpedo (IJN) **14**, 28, **28**, 35, **43**, 60, 66, **67**, **72**, 74, 79
        Type 95 (IJN) 28

Yamamoto, Adm Isoroku 5, 8, **10**, 12, 31, **32**, 43, 44, 53, 54, 55, 61–64, **61**, 75, 76–77
Yushiro, Cmdr Wada 40